Praise for Patricia Jabbeh \

Patricia Jabbeh Wesley is one of th
of the twenty-first century. With iour collections of poetry
spanning over fifteen years, and having won prestigious
awards and garnered rave reviews, she is the most renowned
of African women poets... Jabbeh Wesley occupies a meto-
nymic position in writings about Africa, a continent that has
experienced brutal historic traumas, but one that has an
abundant will to heal, to live, and to flourish...
    —Chielozona Eze, *Interdisciplinary Literary Studies*, (2014)

Praise for *When the Wanderers Come Home*

In Patricia Jabbeh Wesley's powerful *When the Wanderers Come
Home*, the search for a place of arrival, self-recognition and re-
membrance continues, but doesn't find a resting place...
Wesley pays particular tribute to women's resilience, from the
South African protest singer Miriam Makeba whose band's
records sounded "as though its players were born playing" to
an ode to Hurricane Sandy, in which she jokes that "A woman
by herself is category 7 hurricane." There are further works
written on journeys to and from Colombia, Libya, America
and Morocco, but at heart *When the Wanderers Come Home* is
a grieving love letter to Liberia, a country that contains her
story just as she tries to contain all its stories, woman and
country intertwined like "branches and limbs of the same
oak" ("When Monrovia Rises")...
    —Bidisha, *The Poetry Society*, UK

In Wesley's poetry we see the immense power of a poet work-
ing to express the human complexity and grief of a nation
and her people often defined by war.
    —Matthew Shenoda, *World Poetry Today*

Praise for *Where the Road Turns*

With each new volume, her voice grows stronger as it blends
with those of Ama Ata Aidoo, Alda do Espírito Santo, and
Jeni Couzyn. She is without doubt among the most powerful
of the younger generation of African poets.
    —Frank M. Chipasula

Wesley possesses a distinctive, lyrical gift of the highest order.... The emotional appeal of her poetry is direct and accessible. She also has a dramatic gift and a masterly command of place.
—Robert H. Brown, *Liberian Studies Journal*

Praise for *The River Is Rising*

Patricia Jabbeh Wesley's poetry is heartfelt, wise, and alive.... One senses in her that rare combination of someone who has been deeply schooled in both literature and life, and who has integrated those two into a deeply felt and shrewd worldview.
—Stuart Dybek

Patricia Jabbeh Wesley's *The River Is Rising* is both brilliant and heartbreaking. Survivor of the brutal Liberian Civil War, Wesley bears witness to a life she lost to that war, and to what it means to be a refugee who has remade herself...."To every war," she says simply, "There are no winners".... I am in awe of these beautiful, necessary poems, and the glory and largesse of Wesley's vision.
—Cynthia Hogue

Praise for *Becoming Ebony*

This second book also has something of the incantatory nature of Celan's poetics, in which the sheer repetition of certain phrases and ideas points out the irresolution in the mind of a survivor.... Part of the strength of this collection is that it does not allow itself to wallow in the bleakness of this sentiment, but instead confronts and examines the power of death and suffering.... In almost every section of the book, the reader is faced both with the brutal realities of life in parts of the world, and the lyric's possibilities for delineating a space that can act against them.
—*Publishers Weekly*

Wesley writes with clear-eyed lyricism about her ruthless and beleaguered homeland, and the bittersweet relief and loss of the diaspora. Her poems are scintillating and vivid, quickly sketched fables shaped by recollections of childhood play-mates, moonlight and ocean surf, hibiscus hedges, and big pots of boiling soup. But these paeans to home blend with percussive visions of falling rockets and murdered children, sharp recollections of hunger and mourning, and a survivor's careful gratitude in a land of cold winds and rationed sunlight, her carefully measured memories and cherished dreams of return.

—*Booklist* (starred review), Spotlight on Black History

Praise for *Before the Palm Could Bloom: Poems of Africa*

Wesley brings us frontline poetic reportage in *Before the Palm Could Bloom,* her first collection. Many of the voices in this book speak only here.

—*Publishers Weekly*

This book is a tour-de-force testament to the responsibility of writer to witness. She balances the horrors of the Liberian Civil War, from 1989 to 1996—child soldiers and atrocities, almost almost a quarter million dead, three quarter million refugees—against the pastoral legacy of Liberian Life."

—Vince Gotera, *North American Review*

PRAISE SONG FOR MY CHILDREN

New and Selected Poems

PRAISE SONG FOR MY CHILDREN

New and Selected Poems

Patricia Jabbeh Wesley

AUTUMN HOUSE PRESS

Pittsburgh

Autumn House Press receives state arts funding support through a grant from the Pennsylvania Council on the Arts, a state agency funded by the Commonwealth of Pennsylvania, and the National Endowment for the Arts, a federal agency.

Cover art: Nowik Sylwia/Shutterstock.com; © Can Stock Photo Inc./Pablonis
Cover and book design: TG Design

ISBN: 978-1-938769-50-4
Library of Congress Control Number: 2019944861

*This book is dedicated to the beautiful young people
I call my children & many more:*

Ade-Juah, Ade, Besie-Nyesuah, Mlen-Too, Gee, Nmanoh, Amaka,
Francess, Jee-won, Ger, Aaron, Angie, Ashanti, Tendai, Ifeoma,
Vermon, Patricia, Causyl, Fatu, Zawadi, Pallath, Nyonsuate,
Godspower, Tsitsi, Marvin, Sadel, Samel, Sadala, Samela, Ketaki,
Enock, Bei Qi, Kulah, Laurel, Bipasha, Martee, Brooke, Cece Muna,
Gabby, Blair, Lucy, Kasey, Sarah, Beleah, Wlue, Latta, Katherine,
Salma, Palesa, Adokor, Monsio, Taneh, Gbonu, Momolu, Maria,
Erin, Uchenna, Dominic, Monoj, Abi, George, Michael, Mosarraf,
Marcos, Queen, Gonche, Maryam, Norris, Saudia, Samuel, Ransom,
Wyne, Kpana, Doede, Dorme, Chee, Kojo, Ziphozakhe, Kwadi,
Klon, Decontee, Allison, Kweadi, Marie, Ruan, Ruiz, Lois, Samantha,
Kayla, Kenya, Dominique, Quincy, Olalekan, Page, Payton, Siyana,
Briana, Ruth, Marionna, Bianca, Kelvin, Sebastian, Chinedu,
Benjamin, Adia, Rachel, Alexa, Gokce, Jayveer, Keith, Amari,
Elizabeth, Madison, Coralie, Tweade, Dierdre, Eunice, Grace,
Teetee, Nana, Chintin, Jee-hyea, Ayouba, Thelma, Kerry, Alexander,
Wulu, Tyler, Beullah, Whit, Afua, Kudeh, Laurel, Frances, Madella,
Chee, Willie, Ransom, Michael, Gabriel, Allison, Othniel, Lahai,
Winnie, Willtricia, Essah, Wyne, Salma, *and all the other children, our
children across the world. May the roads you follow be kind to you.*

We are characters now other than before
The war began, the stay-at-home unsettled
By taxes and rumor, the looter for office
And wares, fearful everyday the owners may return....

From "Casualties,"
—JOHN PEPPER CLARK-BEKEDEREMO

TABLE OF CONTENTS

III *from* WHERE THE ROAD TURNS (2010)

IV *from* The River Is Rising (2007)

V *from* BECOMING EBONY (2003)

VI *from* BEFORE THE PALM COULD BLOOM (1998)

Foreword by Matthew Shenoda

In Patricia Jabbeh Wesley's *Praise Song for My Children: New and Selected Poems*, we are introduced to the breadth of a poet who has been engaged in a quiet urgency and desire for liberation that she has cultivated as a poet for more than two decades. Hers is a freedom song for home, for woman, for child, for self, a desire rooted in the exploration of how we make sense of our complicated realities and how we move towards a place where we can respect the fullness of our collective humanities. Wesley, a Liberian woman who has dealt with the horrors and aftermath of two civil wars in her lifetime, is perpetually excavating with an aim to discover and rediscover how we remake ourselves; she writes, "no matter how ugly they say home looks, / there's never a day when you do not want to go back home." And it is that yearning for return, not just to place, but to self that drives her poems, that drives her constant sense of unearthing "the irony of tradition that kills itself, / the irony of the forgotten peoples we wail."

But perhaps what is most striking about the work of Patricia Jabbeh Wesley is her ability to be rooted in a place that has suffered tremendously, yet still see the ways she can germinate and re-root herself, her family, and her community in meaningful ways that carry forward tradition and ancestry while creating anew. Her poems teach us that lineage is never a stagnant thing, but an unending expansion, a subtle and often painful growing into, that holds at its core the root of unforgetting. As she states in the title poem "Praise Song for My Children," "I am becoming the calabash / that was not shattered in the shattering." It is that shattering that shapes so much of her work but does not singularly define it. There is a glorious and delicate balance found here, a hope in suffering, and a joy in continuation. In many ways, Wesley has become the poetic "Keeper of the homestead, without whom there's no home." Her remembering of Liberia and her keeping of it through her verse is a kind of nation-work that exemplifies for us the necessity of story-keepers and the possibilities of consequential connections regardless of geography.

Wesley's verse, as is true of so many who have found themselves in diaspora, is "stranded between the future / and our unforgiving history" much like the Paramount Chief she writes of. But unlike the Chief, she is conscious of this stranding and is working tirelessly to find new paths forward. And that path is shaped in large part by a vision of the world rooted in a clear sense of African feminism. Wesley's work is unabashedly Woman, steeped in an understanding that her power as woman, mother, lover, and matriarch are not depleted no matter how others may define her. Hers is a clarity of agency and power that drives her aesthetic leanings and helps give definition to a voice often spoken over. You hold in your hands a necessary map, not only to a place and a history, but to a future that will be defined by the voices that have traditionally been estranged and this is cause for celebration!

I

PRAISE SONG FOR MY CHILDREN
New Poems, 2017-2019

Some of Us Are Made of Steel

Some of us are made of steel.
Some of us are made of twigs. Some of us break
in order to stand and rise above the bend.
Some of us bend and wobble and rock
to the rhythm of all the scars we pick up

as the roads wind us in their hard grip, and toss
us up in the cold, sometimes, hot air
against the dashing against the walls of life.
Some of us are made of jelly, soft to the touch,
but when life gives us a blow, we slide

and glide, and before you know it, we've made
it to the other side away from destruction,
surviving the punches only jelly could take.
Some of us are made of tears,
tears, tears, and we weep hard so rain

falls on hardened, drought-weary soil,
and then the rivers swell and swell and swell,
because somehow, life has made us cry.
But in our tears, salt, healing, salty, and forever,
we are forever. Yes, some of us are forever.

No matter what you toss at us, we rise
again and again and again, like that old river
in my backyard at home, that river that rises,
and we say, oh, the river, and then it goes away,
and we say, oh, the swamp. Some of us are hard,

sometimes, the river, sometimes, the rock.

Praise Song for My Children

Let me be your *Mami Wata*, your River Gee,
crossing you into old Grebo country,
after the hills give way, after the truck slides through
mud and rocks, through dangerous muddy ditches
along Zwedru's lost forest
in search of our fathers' homelands.

Let me be your Mama Africa, your Mama
that grew out of old streams of old rivers
from Kehlebo to Karlorkeh, all the way to Tugbakeh.
Where after so long, only small roosters
remain in a town that used to be ours.

Let me come to you at dawn, my children,
my calabash, wet from the early dawn's
water-fetching-run, my *lappa*, wet from the brush,
from the cry of old pepper birds,
the owl's howling, from the old footpaths lost
to the wanderer's feet.
Let me come to you bearing tears on my face
after the war, after the villages have crumbled
under the weight of grave hate.

Let me be your landfill, your garbage dump,
the one, only who could carry you in her young,
supple womb, carrying you with my youth,
carrying you, even though Liberia was losing
herself, and from afar, we could see
the oncoming smoke of war.
Let me come to you, bearing palm branches
that weathered too quickly in the heat of March.
Here, take from my hand, and drink, my child,
one by one, take and drink.
After the afterbirths have parched hard
in the soil where we did not bury them.
After our feet have become parched from running,
after our way back home has been burned by war,
let me be your *Mami Wata*,
your Mama, rising out of the wild ocean tide.

4

Let me be your consolation
that the land I gave to you is dying.

I am becoming an old woman, now, my sons.
I am becoming my mother and her mother's mother.
I am becoming the ghosts of my mothers
I am becoming *Iyeeh*, bowlegged,
I am becoming fire and rain.
I am becoming *Sebo*.
I am becoming the water-bearer.
I am becoming the calabash
that was not shattered in the shattering.

Let me sing to you, my daughters, you who have,
never known where we come from.
You who will never know your mother's tongue,
you who have become the metaphor of lost
warriors, who were captured by war.
Let me be your songwriter, the song you sing,
the dirge you do not know how to sing.

Let me wrap around you, my *lappa* that has been
lost in the storm. Let me lay down
all my *lappas* for you to walk on,
my blood-soiled *lappas* from the war.
Let me come to you, my daughters, when the sun
becomes yellow and then red, when it seems
the sun is falling down upon us.

Let me come to you, carrying the moon
in my warm palms. Let me be your *Mami Wata*,
your one Mama, rising out of the waves of war.
Let me be your road map home.
Let us walk together homeward, where the ocean
roars in peace and in war, the rising tides
along Liberia's coast.
Let me be your tears.
Let me be the Mesurado.

When I rise at dawn, my children, I long for you,
but I long for home more.
I long for a lost country that I seek to know again.
When I rise, my sons, I long for the sound of the drum
that used to sit at *Tuwah-Kai.*
I long for cassava shoots and for the banana tree
to bloom again. I long for me.
I long for the girl that was lost.
I long to find my feet again, to find my feet again,
to find my feet again.

I long to be me.
Let me come to you, carrying hope in my hands.
Let me come to you carrying hope in my hands.
Let me come to you, my daughters,
carrying hope in my hands.

GRACE

God sends grace, every day. Sometimes, grace
is a poem, written by a friend or two to me.
Sometimes, a small note, a ray of sunlight
through cracked blinds.

Sometimes, a laugh in my own throat, burnt
sauce, discovered before the house finally caught
fire, sometimes, a phone call from a long-
lost friend,

an almost fender bender, a honk from
an oncoming car or a man wobbling over
his cane, looking up to say hi. Sometimes,
it is just the rain,

heavy drops against my willing window glass.
Sometimes, it is cancer, refusing to grow,
a tumor, pinned against my hardening
uterine wall

after all the babies have exited, are now in college
and finding their own open roadways and roadblocks.
Sometimes, grace is a soft song in the morning,
on my phone,

the phone, now made to sing to us all the hymns
we've forgotten in the new foggy weather
of our lives. Sometimes, grace
is just rolling out of bed.

I Saw Men Leaving My Mother

I saw men leaving my mother.
I saw them beat her bloody red and bruised,

their rough, dusty hands, and one by one,
I saw them packing up their ugly rags. I saw them

in their khaki pants, their rugged shirts, coming
home from garbage jobs over the years, over

the dirty, rocky soil that was Monrovia. Hard, hot,
melting tarred roofs, where the poor squatted

and waited and waited as if poverty were a thing
like October rain, fleeting and quickly forgotten.

I saw them beat her with hard fists, her face,
bruised, and I saw her when my Mama fell on

her knees, begging one useless, cheap,
gin-smelling man to stay, to please forgive her,

to stay and beat her some more. The 1960s,
somewhere in the middle of that ugly decade.

I was around eight or nine, and my brother, Sunday,
five or six, the two of us awakened from sleep

by the pounding of our Mama, who dropped
out of school a teenager, almost a decade earlier

just to carry me in her womb, to nurture my being
into being, to bring me into the world, and I was

now standing in the middle of our small room
in the middle of night in the middle of Monrovia.

With my birth, poverty was bestowed upon our
Mama like the will of a mean father. I saw her try

to hold on, one man after the other all her life, my
Mama, weeping, trying to be somebody's woman.

I saw her praying at dawn and at dusk because
there was no food. I saw her finally at middle age,

the warrior woman, now weary, only the sparkle
in her big eyes, all her possessions loaded

onto my uncle's old truck, that final leaving.
This time, it was not the man leaving.

FIRE AND RAIN
for my father, Moses

I want to hold on to the parts of my father
that are not fading into the night.
That broad smile, the hard laugh, the frown,
the stern twist of face, the disapproving eye
when a neighbor boy who thought he'd fallen

in love is caught sitting with me in our living
room; my father, his white delicately starched
shirt, buttoned close to his Adam's apple.
I want to hold on not to shirts or to his always black
framed glasses, but to the hope in those huge

balding eyes, which when he was sixty, made me
think Pa was so hardworking, he could fall asleep
standing. I want to fold me in his dream of me, walking
down a road no other woman had walked.
Hope was not a fading cloud in my father's eyes.

I saw in him, something hard and forever, like ebony,
like an oak, like walnut, standing alone at *Gbaliahde,*
where at birth, they planted his umbilical cord
just so he would become the mighty tree that he was.
My father, the lion, *Kwadi Chee,* eater of fresh
leaves, the king, the elders called him.

I want to hold on to his life forever since a father
did not die, did not get buried before his eldest
girl-child could see him lie in death in his casket,
clasped hands, his face still held high; even in death,
a father did not fade into cloud and dust.

I want to hold on to his phone number forever,
to hold it captive in my phone forever,
to hold on to his sharp voice, his early
morning calls, pleading like a dying friend,
begging me to come home for his dying.

His pleading surprise about the reasons
his eldest girl-child could not come home
the way a daughter was supposed to, and his not
knowing why I would not say why.
But how does a daughter tell her dying

father that she is too ill to walk, that
a cancer patient does not pull out steroid tubes,
does not pull out chemo filled tubes to wail
loud on a long flight across the Atlantic?
How do you tell your dying father that you

cannot come? But in my heart, I'll hold on
to his last sharp laugh, the giving up
and not giving up when at last he knew it
without knowing. That acceptance of finality,
the negotiation between the eldest daughter

and the dying father, where the huge Atlantic
stands wide, the negotiation of burial rites,
that goodbye even as his voice held strong,
the concession in that last "I'm proud of you,
my daughter," the final word from a man

as tough as a steel rock from Tugbakeh, Father,
the early morning dew catcher, the road map
from Kaluway, my father, leaving me to take
the journey where the journey wants to go.
My father, fire and rain, my father, Moses,

parting the Red Sea so the sons of Kaluway
could follow, the bookman, parting
brush and forest. Moses, *Kwadi Chee*,
father of fathers, I want to hold you forever.

Praise Song for Sister Marie Morais-Garber

Sister Marie, Himie Yude, a woman among women,
at home, the Grebo people call you "The Great One,"
Nyene-Wheh, mother of children, mother of mothers,
the one without whom a child cries out for love.
Keeper of the homestead, without whom there's no home.

Khade-Wheh, we greet you, mother, sister, wife,
the one upon whose hands a home stands firm.
Some people are forever, that one person who stands
with you when everyone else has abandoned you
the way birds abandon forest and farm for better pastures.

In college, you were my inspiration that a woman
could be all, woman and hero and mother and wife.
That a woman could pick up the pieces of her life
and be anything she wanted to be. You were the one
I thought of when I dreamed big, but you didn't know

it, my own sister shero, you didn't know this, Sister
Marie G, mother and wife and friend and pillar
and warrior woman all in one. After all these years,
I open my mailbox, and there it is, you who never
forget that I have a birthday even though I have

forgotten my own birthday. A phone call, traveling
across ocean miles in defiance, and your soft voice,
still gracious, still warm, still filled with love
for a sister like me who often forgets to be a smaller
sister, oh, my own Sister Marie, the older sister

I never had, and here I am, Grebo woman to Grebo
woman, asking you, how much love can one woman
carry at her breast, how many people can she enclose
in those arms, how many years, how many times?
Oh, how I love you for who you are, Marie G,

Joe Garber's girl, Grebo woman, still beautiful and smart
and loving, and yes, he said, "MMG" on your license
plate was for "Meet My Girl," and yes, we have met
you, and since we did, we have never been the same,
Marie G, Sister Marie, mother of mothers, Great One.

NOVEMBER 12, 2015

for Liberia

November 12, thirty years after our failed coup,
and I am driving through another city.
Hills, valleys, old houses clinging to years gone.

I've been an alien so long,
sometimes I feel like belonging.

But the ground here is gray, soft, clay rocks
in between white soil, clay enough to turn soil
into pots and plates into jugs.

Difference is measured not only in the cold
November frost, the falling leaves
or in the slow yellowing of oak
even though we know that no matter
how long it takes the oak

to yellow and turn red like fire, red like blood,
no matter how stubborn its will,
the oak will shed its leaves like
all the other trees, become as brittle
as dry limbs after a forest fire.

November 12, and my mind takes me way back home.
Home, the humid sun, bright, hot, like fire,

and the town, divided by the ocean
and the river, the past of bloodshed,
the burning anger and pain, when years
ago, a hero came, or shall
we call him coward? Thomas Quiwonkpa,

coup planner, or shall we call him the messenger
of death, sent by alien people
to rob us of home? Liberia, fire, death,
the massacre of our people, the beginning
of the rest of our lives in exile.

November 12, as I drive through this strange town,
where for years, my heart has longed for home,

the early morning mist, rising out of the Mesurado,
the honking cars, the market women on their way
to work, and out of nowhere, my neighbors'
voices, shouting at another hard day.

November 12, but this is where a road leads home,
the earth, red, blood and water, my family line

where the soil still holds onto my umbilical cord,
buried in the hills of Dolokeh, home, and Monrovia,
where my father's grave awaits my return
so I can kneel and cry and pray, and tell him how
sometimes, I am so lonely in this far away country,
I want to walk and walk and walk and walk
and walk until I'm back home again.

November 12, no matter how ugly they say home looks,
there's never a day when you do not want to go back home.

The New Year: 2018

The new year comes upon us, icicles and snow-
storms, the cold, banging winds against my house,

whistling, howling as if the wind knows something
we do not know, and somehow in our jubilation

of the crossover from the tired, old year, we
forget that the road ahead may be bumpy, sad,

and unforgiving. And no one has prepared us
for the journey, and it is only the idea of the trip

we carry in our bags of worries as we pound
our feet in celebration of an unassuming new year.

As if we were children again on a car ride, we think
we know what awaits us at the end of the road,

or how our year will evolve, and we think we know
that the hills ahead will be flattened for us,

or that we know its turns, the winding way down
at the crossroads. Is this because we are human,

knowing, as human as we are? Or is it faith?
Faith, in its rawness like steel, the need to know

that none of us will perish in this new year
as new as a new friend, the dark morning hour,

the midnight before the dawning of the day, the new
friend we do not truly know, cannot know the way

a checked baggage handler knows the bags he tosses
onto a plane. On the phone, my husband says

the new year looks the same in Harper, like the year
an hour ago. Outside his window, it is dark, Liberia,

crickets chirping as always, and up the road
at the Cape, Harper is still dying. Abandoned city,

old buildings, moist air, and the ocean banging
against shoreline as it has done for hundreds

of years, old mansions knowing abandonment like
a woman knows abandonment. The once living city,

dead like crabs on what once was a living beach,
the hard hand of war having robbed the city of itself

and its people year after another new year. All that we
used to know is today rusted, even as we celebrate.

Holding Back

After so many years, I've learned how to hold back,
to give you only a portion of my heart,
to take it back, take back the years I gave you
so many years ago when we were young, and when
our eyes sparkled in the reflection of glass.

To hold on to my heart you often left along the roads
you and I learned to walk, to hold myself back
between these my now aging hands
like a woman holds to her newborn, to take
the years and make of them what you could not
let me make of them, to relive,
to breathe breath into this old me.

I am an African woman after all, my darling.
I am becoming *Iyeeh*, becoming my mother,
becoming the tears of her losses,
becoming the abandonment my mother knew,
becoming her aging self.
I am becoming the ground my feet tread,
becoming the leaf, she did not let fall,
becoming the woman, we are, my darling,
becoming all those African women
who learned to hold up the fort despite the smoke,
despite the hut burning of want of love,
becoming the embodiment of our joint anger.
I have become the metaphor
of the pain of our ancestral mothers.

I'm learning to say no, to stand a ground other girls
still cannot, to stand their ground for them,
to refocus my pupils, to rebuild me,
to find me among the rubble we left
behind at home. I have learned that love
is like a passing wave and that a wave
is like love and that we cannot possess the wind
no matter how rich or poor we are,
and that life is only breath,
and that the love the wind brings is unreal.

After all these years, I've learned that if the heart
has been broken so many times and mended again
and again, it leaves cracks in between places
where no matter how hard you try,
there is still that leak forever. Or is it my mind
that is leaking into my head or my head
into my mind or my heart into the head of my being?
My heart is taking back not just the lost years,
my darling, but in between the lost years,
those times when I was so young, I took
out my brain, and on a platter, gave it to you.

I'm taking that back also with the years,
all the good and the sad memories,
as if a log that was tossed on the water years ago
is returning to its town, emptied of mud.
All the sad memories came back to haunt
me like the way a dead man returns
to a town that killed him.
All the memories of you being lost, you, losing
yourself, and not knowing how to find yourself
as I sought to find you again.
Love that is lost, when is returned is scarred
and bruised and wounded, and it is
so hard to put that love back together.

Every time the present reminds me that it is new,
this thing, this love that was stolen by loose women,
this love that wandered until it lost itself,
when it came back to me, I was gone.
I was here and not here.
I had packed up my mind and my woman-being,
my heart, and even now as I seek to unpack
and return to myself and to you again,
something in me is holding back, holding back
like a baby holds back when a lost father
returns to be a father again.

Or when a husband returns to reclaim the wife
he lost in his wanderings between home
and the streets or when the beautiful moon returns
to us, riding under the sun or when the moon hides
behind the sun, that loss, so hard,
like the death of a lover.
There is an eclipse in the heart of things, my old
love, there is an eclipse in our lost love,
when the man you gave your heart returns
like when you first met him,
and you are gone even though you are there,
you are gone, gone like the year,
gone to the river and to the Atlantic.
And you keep on trying to rekindle the fire,
but everything is only a shadow of what once was.
And everything has become a shadow.

AT THE BORDERLINE

In a town at the edge of Grand Gedeh
and River Gee, the red roads wind up
and downhill. We stop for drinks,
and come upon a Paramount Chief seated
on a porch, our dusty red bodies, dusty clothing,
having left behind dozens of cars stuck for miles
in deep mud, the unknowing, coming upon
treacherous roads from Ganta to Harper,
our forgotten homelands.

But the forestlands we used to know are now
depleted and barren. A dying land, a dying people,
a dying country, travelers stranded along the forest
roads for weeks, their goods, rotting in the wait.
Somewhere along the road, travelers are turning
into villagers, roasting cold-water fish over a fire.
These are the scars we've come to break.

But the Paramount Chief tells me he wants
to take my already married niece's hand
for his son, to have him wed and to hold
in these jungle parts.
The Paramount Chief does not want
my dark-skinned unmarried niece.
But these are not the days of our mothers.
These are not the days when a young girl
was given to old, lazy men like goats.
But the dusty red of the roads can be misleading.

The Paramount Chief, red, like the red dust
of the road to Harper. He tells us that Oral
is beautiful because she's red like the road, red,
the way a white girl is red, her light-skinned beauty,
the way his brainwashed mind sees beauty.
The Paramount Chief is not worried that he's been
in darkness forever, that his town
has been forgotten in the gravitational pull
of the sliding of the Krahn Language
as it slowly becomes Grebo.
This last town before the forest picks up

where loggers have depleted our forests.
This is where the civil war has left us, the way
a mother abandons her child.

The Paramount Chief listens to me speak
my Grebo, his eyes, wide.
How is it possible for someone like me
to speak Grebo, he asks, walking away
to get his son to marry my niece
on the forgotten highway to Harper,
on this old road that weaves the unforeseen traveler
into a web of loss, the winding hills, the unpaved
pieces of our lives, the losses of loss, the country
we wail if we know how far we have fallen.

Where a Paramount Chief is not concerned
about his town. The Paramount Chief whose
worries are as tiny as the fireflies we meet
along our journey back to places we fled.
The Paramount Chief, in search of a red woman
for his son, the irony of tradition that kills itself,
the irony of the forgotten peoples we wail.

But our car speeds on sadly, and my mind wanders
to the hundreds, stranded between the future
and our unforgiving history.

MAYBE

Maybe, the trees know they are supposed to go.
Their limbs, folding shutters, as if they had any
shutters to fold, closing up
arms and eyes to the sunshine that is still
blazing from the sky in mid-September,
as if trees were armed with arms and eyes.
The ugly degrees of wet humidity,
and they fold up for the long rest
despite the sun's refusal to go away,
despite the refusal of fall to come back
to this old place, despite the faithfulness
of hurricane winds, tearing up
earth and wind and ocean and everything
we thought we owned, despite us.
The trees know the time and the hour
for their change of color, the change of time,
like that old lover you clung to
in high school, that boy you loved so much
you thought he would become husband
and father of children to come, a keeper,
you thought, but somehow,
he knew it was time to go.
That he was not for you, that he would fail
like limbs of trees, fail like a boy was supposed
to fail because he knew you more
than you knew yourself, that you were
too precious for him, that you were cut out
for bigger dreams, bigger worlds, that he
was the sort that killed women's dreams.
But unlike the trees, he knew that he was
supposed to go and never return.
That he would have killed the spark
in your big brown eyes, and killed you.
The trees know something we cannot know.
Maybe that is why the men we left behind
still stand by the wayside
wondering why they let us go.

They Killed a Black Man in Brooklyn Today
a dirge for our sons

A policeman has just killed a black man
in Brooklyn. Today, another black man,
shot
           and killed

in America, where we must stop our car
so a squirrel can cross a busy highway.
But another policeman in America
has just killed another one of our sons
in Brooklyn.

When my phone alerts me, `
I feel my belly button turning hot.
My legs buckled and I could feel my own
fingers trembling around
the curves of my phone.
Suddenly, I forget my son's number.
I forget the way to call my own son in Brooklyn.
My mind tells me it cannot recall
how to push the buttons so my Brooklyn black
son can assure me
that he is not dead.

To be a black woman is to be a woman,
ready to mourn. To be a black mother
is to go to bed
with your head halfway on your pillow.
To be a black mother in America
is to stand between night and day,
waiting to see if the policeman
will not kill your son today.

They say a black man was shot in a city
so populated by good black men
they now must empty bullets
into another black man.

They say a policeman in Brooklyn has decided
to shoot a black man because there was

a suspect on the run
or because he was holding up something
or because he was taking something
out of his own pocket
or because he was just a black man.
There should be no black men in Brooklyn
if there is a suspect on the run.
There should be no black men in America
when there is a suspect on the run.

When my phone finally remembers
its own number, my son's voice on the line
sounds like I have won the lottery.
But somewhere, a mother has just
lost her son in Brooklyn.

A mother who gave birth to her son is wailing
because there was a suspect on the run.
Today, I saved the life of a scary doe
that ran across my neighborhood road
as if it knew the sound of tires,
the sound of a passing car
the sound of death, the sound a gun makes
before it kills a black man,
before it kills a black man in Brooklyn.

But they say we must not count.
And they say we do not count.
One black man was killed today in Brooklyn,
but on TV, there is no news.
There is no news of the black man, killed
in Brooklyn.
On TV, white people are talking about
white people.

But somewhere all over America, a black man
will be shot the way
a black man was shot in Brooklyn.
On TV, white people are talking
about white problems.
While a black man swallows a bullet.
While a bullet swallows the life
of a black man in America.

ON SEPTEMBER 11
a memorial to the unknown

On September 11, I always think of the homeless
and all those unknown, the forgotten, street people,
those who sit in alleyways, on the stairways,

those who belong to nobody, the forgotten we see
along street corners, their shabby coats unfolding
stories we're too busy to read, their eyes, sunken

and alone, the aloneness of our manufactured world,
enfolding them as they wait as if waiting for us
or for tomorrow or for a god under the shadows

of buildings so built of steel, we thought they were
invincible, those with no name, whose names will
never grace a stone or wall or the lips of a grieving

mother or child or wife, those who were forgotten
in the count, the beggars, too ashamed to be beggars
until that morning when the first plane flew into

the first tower, and looking up, the second also fell,
the homeless with his old coat torn at the sleeve, his
food in a small cart he toted around a city so alive,

the city forgot him, and I wonder how Heaven
remembers such heroes, and even as they ascended
into the Heavens, I wonder if somehow, the rich

and the poor, the homeless, the unknown coffee boy
at the corner bar, the unknown child who fled home
away from family until family forgot he was still

alive, and I wonder if the rising dead held hands, poor,
rich, the beloved and the unloved, and all those who
shaped the world before the world shattered us all,

and how I wonder how it felt holding hands like us
in our common tragedy, the gone, and those whose
bodies were so crushed, but in death, they rose

and rose above their killing, the beloved father
and the motherless run-away child, the street walker,
the black, the white, and the yellow skin?

Since no matter who we are, dying is dying,
the common denominator since blood is blood
and grief is as deep as grief and all our tears flow

all the same, and the heart pounds like a heart
in grief and in pain, no matter who we say we are.
I wonder as we remember, if they remember us.

The Unbuckling: A Dirge
November 9, 2016

Does anyone else feel like they've lost a loved one, lost
their mother, the other end of their umbilical cord?

Lost their blood root, their link to tubers that have
forcefully stretched underground for years,

their crisscrossing roots of underground family part,
like losing their childhood friend, their sister-kin,

that hard loss, like the dashing against a hard thing?
That loss of freedom, a tragedy of some sort, an

undoing of many decades of freedom, the unfolding
of a great hold, an unbuckling of tired steel knuckles

against steel, the loosening of what was, this freedom
that in the palm of a refugee is fine diamonds, sparkling,

after the dark of war? Oh, I can't bring myself to shake
off this mourning. My friends, come, freedom died

last night. Lay out the mourning cloths, lay out many
mourning *lappas*, lay them out in the dark morning dew.

Even the sun will not come out to meet us this morning.
The sun does not want to look us in the face after

this election oh, give me a piece of cloth, a large towel
so I can wail my pain, oh, my people, who will help me

grieve this grief? Lay out many black *lappas* end to end,
lay them out in the early morning dew until the night

rescues this reluctant sun. Lay them out so the mourning
women can sit and cry dirges for this great loss, oh, how

did we stumble so hard? Oh, did they go out and sell
our hopes for thirty pieces of silver, ah-ah? But they say

this is a free country-o, home of the free, where other
tens of millions looked into the eye of a piece of paper

and darkened it with their hate, but is that what they call
voting, and did they paint it so they didn't have to see

the dark of my skin, their scratching that made all that
evil of the man seem so good? Did we lose our way

into the long ago ugly past, oh, how my blood ripples
within my dark blood. Maybe I'll wake up to hating people

someday, like staring at the white person at the red
light, and going, *I wonder if she/he was* among

the percentage of those. I'm glad I know you know
I know you voted for him, but it's all the other millions,

like the man tailgating me yesterday, his Trump flag
flying above one side of his truck, and on the other,

the Confederate flag. The good news is the bad news
of our common loss. The bad news is the good news

of our awakening. I think I'm writing a poem. I can see
the lines on my page, long lines across our cities, people

of all shades, marching, lines of the undoing of this
injustice, lines in protest because we are not a people

void of strength. We will unbuckle each biting pain
of such a woeful day. We will unshackle each shackle.

Too Many Chickens Are Coming
Home to Roost

Let us open the doors. Let us lift the shutters
over the thresholds of the doors; let us
remove the bars from the door posts,
too many chickens are coming home to roost,

and it is not the storm. It is not August
or September hurricane. It is not the storm
that's driving home all the angry of heart,
all the hate that, like aged tar on broken

pavement, has lifted onto the roads, and now,
too many chickens are coming home to roost.
Let us open the doors not to let them in.
Let us open the doors to let us out.

Do not turn down your lights. Do not go to
bed with your eyes closed. Do not let your young
sons out. Do not wander into unknown places.
Do not listen to the wind. Too many roosters

have come home to drive us away from town.
We who came running from the fires
of our homelands have been told to flee again.
Too many roosters have come home to roost

because hate is not a thing we can hold
in a sieve. Hate is not a thing we can place a finger
upon to soothe away hurt. Hate is as hard
as a burning stone, as hard as pain, as an open sore.

AFTER THE ELECTION

After the election, we will hold hands again
and be black and white, again, and lie together
in bed without the world banging at us, banging
the brains of our bodies into us not being us.

After the election, we can go back again into
the world, where an earthquake killed hundreds,
and yet we didn't want to know it, and we don't care
after all, there is the election news, bigger than

the world, where we have turned into a faraway
island of us and us. After the election, we can
call up the friend we lost in the pile of rubble
when the earthquake of hate dug deep scars

like graves, where we buried love and peace.
And now, all around us are enemies we cannot
know. After the election, we shall walk upright,
lift our heads, say hi, without a heavy heart

or maybe, with a heavy heart. We shall become
not white or black or dark or even not a Muslim
or maybe not, maybe not, I say. Maybe, after
the election, we shall need boats with ropes

to pull us out of the flooding of dark rivers
of hate, maybe, we shall now carry not just a
rifle, not only an automatic bullet-spitting gun,
but machetes and bombs since the election

was not about a leader, but about something
like a storm that uproots not only the trees, but a
whole town. After the election, maybe, maybe,
we will put away our bile of speech, our anger,

our lies about the swamp that was not a swamp.
Maybe, we shall go out and see our neighbor again,
maybe, a picnic, maybe again, we shall hold hands
with someone of the other, maybe, maybe not.

Poem Written from Failed Chat Notes

"Hi PJ," someone writes, the PJ, calmer than
the owner of the name. I love to see my initials
so free of all the cares of earthly possessions.
"Looking for job," another writes, just like
that, looking for a job. The message is flat,
like a pan, no, no, like a flat board, where
the cutting of potatoes further flattens
the map where the job may be found.

"Hello," the echo, clearly discernible
through the pressing of keys, this time,
a woman, out there in Southeast Asia, "Hello,"
she says, as if words were sufficient
in themselves to return to us, filled
with air bubbles, like a balloon.

"Hello, madam," one man says like a sigh,
carrying the silence that only the word,
"madam," can leave behind. I check him out,
and his hair, combed back as if after shower.
Somewhere in India, it is hot now.
"How r you today?" Another adds,
as if to complete the sentence
others have left hanging
on the tiny lines of these long distance
greetings, like litter on the page of a phone.

"Hi, how r u?" Another interjects, and as
quickly as that came in, here comes
another, in correction of grammar, I guess,
"How are u today?" So I think, we should
all agree that the proper spelling of "you"
has to be "u." But before I linger too long
on whether "u" is better than "you,"
here comes another, more elaborate,
a lecture on the art of caring,
something I needed to hear today.

But when I do not respond, another comes
in, maybe to take back his long discourse,
he says, simply and calmly, "Hello."
I love the word better. "Hello." At least, I can
write a poem with that. Hello, hello, imagine
a poem with a hundred hellos all over the
page, a hundred and fifty hellos.

When the next greeting stops at something
like, "Hello, big sis," I step away from
the computer to check my weight.
For a moment, I think he means "big,
fat, overweight, large," what can I say
to another brother of mine far across
the ocean somewhere? I love Facebook's
ability to tie us through air and space
by hanging strings and names.

After a while, I'm tired of reading.
All across the message inbox are fragments
of disconnected thoughts unending,
the fracturing of thoughts by people who
could be otherwise, fractured. So, like
pieces of jumbled up thoughts, I read on
and on, "Patricia," "Hi," "Mm," "Hey,"
"Hello, mam," "Good morning," "hey,"
"Wat's up?" "Oh," "Mam," "What's up?"
In between the carefully incompleteness

of language, are those whose stories no one
will tell. I wish I knew the next sentence,
the twisting of a finger on a small keyboard
just to scribble a single word. Someday,
there will be strings of words strung together
so another can complete the thoughts of another.
I love you all, I say to myself, but most of all,
I love the incompleteness with which
you complete the things you cannot say.

The Meeting Place

In the restroom, a young teen twists
and turns at the mirror.

Adjusts her hair, and then again
adjusts her hair.

She needs her two hands to reposition
her hips, twisting and more turning.

The one foot out against the emptiness
of space, as if to correct

a figure God must have left undone,
the sins only God commits.

And then for some reason, she notices
this is a public restroom,

that space is carved out unevenly, and her
quick smile at me tells me she knows I'm here with her.

Her grin, like her jeans, torn and conflicted,
her skinny is not so new, and she knows

I know her. I have had her in my life all along,
did give birth to her, pushed her out,

pushed out all of them teens, girls, turning
thirteen; all her life, I have held her

like I have held my daughters, after giving
them life, staring at them after birth,

not knowing there was a day when pants
would be attached to their skins

like the way sin remains with us
even after the confession.

She smiles again after the restoration,
as if to say, "I know you too."

POEM WRITTEN IN MY DOCTOR'S OFFICE

Some mornings I float like a piece of paper in the wind,
pile upon pile, my daily routines stacked against

one another as I juggle children, husband, my life
of teaching, writing, reading useless emails,

I make it through the day, drive home, so I can sink
into a couch in this America where I have unbuckled

myself from extended family, where the Atlantic's
salty winds have twisted rust in between the five

thousand miles, where in the salty time of air
and space, I've lost it all—home, siblings, nieces

and nephews—all strangers. There are no rewards
in the wandering feet of the exile. There is no laughter

when you are so many miles away from your
homeland, and you grope for ropes in the raging

waters between here and Africa. In my dream, I am
a flying angel, carrying the tears of my wandering,

lost ancestors who are beckoning us to come home,
to come on home, to come back home now.

At the doorposts, the kola nut is growing and bleeding
in *Iyeeh's* kola-nut bowl, where the kola nut has grown

small limbs as the old hometown awaits my return.

SUBURBIA

To each, their groundhog,
their slanting rolling hills, their green, green
of endless lawns, and if a house
could bow, there it is, Pennsylvania.
And to each, their heavy SUVs
so the hills can climb higher
or the cars can navigate the hills
of snowy cliffs when winter
arrives, and the groundhog no longer
can bathe under the sun under my trees
under my brush under my underdeck
under my eyeballs under my nerves
· where a backyard can scare
away buyers, fearful their toddler
may someday fall down my groundhog,
cliffs, where a herd of deer may walk freely
up these my cliffs without falling.

As if a toddler were a stand-alone thing,
unhooked to mother unlike a family of deer.
They want me to level the hills
to the level of leveled hills.
They want me to move the house,
to push, to push and push until
the house is pushed farther onto
leveled ground where ground keeps its level.
They want me to level myself to the level
of ground, of brainless days of leveling
everything to the level of unleveled things.
They want this house at the level
of the groundhogs and squirrels
and the only surviving, passing deer.
They want me to level the cost
to the level of wildflowers, to bring
myself to the level of ground.
To each their worries of wealth,
their passing feet of not knowing
who the next-door neighbor is.

To each their quiet movement through
this suburban life of silence, of coldness,
distance amidst the distant hills and the sound
of mowers and engines, the rushing freeway,
rushing nowhere, trucks that never know sleep.
To each, their nothingness, a life of chasing winds,
and finally, age, solitude, lost friends,
nothing. And finally, finally, finally.

TSA Check

One of these days, a black woman's wig will
fall off her head, a black woman's
hair will land at the feet of that TSA woman
who pats our heads
as if she has everything against us.
All that patting down of boobs,
the pushing against aching knees
as if anyone has ever brought down a plane
by inserting bombs under their old knees.
One of these days, all those blonde clipped
hair pieces under my white girlfriend's hair
will also come flying off
at the TSA check, those air blowing
X-ray machines, flying at the head and hair
as if hair had anything to do with bringing a plane
down. One of these days, a wig will take off
like a jet, flying away like a jet.

They come at us like we have done something
wrong for just being people. They come at us
as if the new padded breasts and buttocks
and fake boobs and fake parts of us
were in themselves capable
of hiding bombs and missiles, capable
of bringing a plane down.
They come at us as if they want us
to deposit our breasts at the check-in desk.
How many women have used their wigs to bring
a plane down? How many of us have
even used our jelly breasts to bring down a plane?

Yes, a woman has used her breasts
and her eyes, her big fat butt and her swinging
body parts to bring down a man
from his false height, so many men, going
down like falling jets in a bombing raid,
so many of them falling into deep ditches
losing everything, like Bill Cosby

and all of them men, losing it all, their old
loose selves, losing it all to the power
of a single woman's smile, but a plane and a wig,
they don't mix, and Lord knows
how unstable a wig is to carry a woman's head
under its body, so, how could a wig
carry a bomb? Who told these TSA
people that a wig had such power?
Who trained them to pat down my head anyway?

THE WOMAN NEXT DOOR

for my Sister Sheroes, gone

I was awakened by a gasp, a coughing and puffing
as if something irrepressible was seeking to take

control of something uncontrollable. This was the night
after my own surgery; tubes connected to tubes

everywhere on me, I managed to sit up and push
a button. I wanted something to happen to cut off

that coughing. I wanted someone to come and relieve
that woman next door. But the button I pressed had

become mute. The whole world must have gathered
around her bed, but the coughing lived on and on,

so I sat up in bed, knowing how keeping vigil can help
lead the spirit upward kindly. So, why does a woman

in the room next door die? Why does she have to die
or is she not dying, I wondered. In the morning, there

was an army of people crowded in both my doorway
and hers, a whole troop of her relations, until

the entire hallway was clogged up like an old pipeline.
Maybe, they needed to help her spirit rise. Maybe,

they needed to hold hands around her dead body so
she would return to us someday. Maybe they needed

to be the way we want our children to be while we
are still alive, while we still have eyes to see them

love us, while we still have air in our lungs to breathe.
Afterwards, there was a silence as still as that calm

before a tornado arrives, before a hurricane or that still
moment when the storm has long passed, after the wrecked

houses are bent and tree limbs have given up
their ghosts, and limping over, and the wrecked lives

of the whole town lays wasted and broken and the air,
ashamed of itself and the ground, having been betrayed,

awaits healing. My husband, down the hall, is blocked
by her army. I sit in my bed waiting, and finally,

my husband comes in, looking like someone who has
come out of the rain, unsoiled. He looks at me as

if relieved that I was still alive. He stares into my eyes
as if to say, "She's gone," but on his lips, no words.

Maybe he saw her stretcher wheeled away. Maybe, he
saw her family in tears. When I later tell him about

the coughing woman, he stares ahead, "She's gone,"
he says, my fellow cancer patient next door, gone.

An Elegy for Art Smith

Some days were created out of the womb of a woman
only for grieving, for the flow of tears, for sitting
with your hands on your lap,
just shaking your head because you've just lost
a dear loved one.
Today is that sort of day, so gloomy, all the darkness
of earth, coming out of the wounds
of unspent years in protest against death.
If this were in the evening, the stars
would not come out. This is when the moon
stands still, when children decide to tease
the moon and make it follow them.
But the moon does not follow because
something as horrible as death has happened.
This is when even a metaphor stands in awe
between a doorway and its own door.

I am in grief, Art, that you are dead.
That you died three days ago, died the way
a poem dies in its own heart, died, the way blankets
fold themselves after their owner
takes leave of them, finally, the way birds fly
South, the way the hills collapse after days
of torrential rainfall.
That dying only a poet does because
after all their words have broken through
the doors of many hearts, they take leave
as if they didn't say a word
to push off the call of death.

Art Smith, I did not know you before you came
like fresh wind at dawn, drawn only by poetry
or like leaves fly in search of new ground,
after fall's strong winds toss them into your yard.
The news say you are no more, Art, that you are gone,
the way we lose everything, the way
we lose ourselves, the way words are lost
from lips, the way our world folds under us.

But you are not dead, buddy.
You are only gone from us and from the body
of things as we see them with our bare eyes.
You are here, in this room, where I sit,
laboring over your poem. You are alive,
dear Art, as the wind lives on.

When I Meet My Ancestors

When my ancestors come to greet me
at the outskirts of the other world,
I will be carrying in my hands, all the bags
of leaves the wind has brought me
from my neighbor's yard.

When I cross over the threshold into the other
world, my ancestors will wonder
what it is I am carrying.

When I greet my ancestors, I will tell them
how my life has been littered by falling
leaves, falling dreams, falling skies.
I will tell my Fathers about a journey
they did not know I would take.
It is not the leaves alone I will be carrying.
It is not the heartache of living so far
away from home I will be carrying.
It is not just the tears in a pail I will be carrying.
It is not just the sore feet the wanderer carries
I will be bringing.

When I meet my Mothers, they will sit
me down on *The Mat* to wipe my eyes.
When I meet my Mothers, they will sit
me down on *The Mat*
and wipe my eyes.
When I meet my mother,
she will sit me on her lap, and wipe my eyes.
When I meet my mother, she will sit
me on her lap, and with her *lappa*,
she will wipe my eyes.
When I meet my mother, she will take
from my tired hands, this bundle of rotten
leaves and the pail of tears
I have brought to her.

When I meet my mother, she will sit
me in the middle of the room
just like she did when I came home
after years away at boarding school.
When I meet my mother,
she will sit me on her lap, and with her
lappa, she will dry my tears.

II

Poems from:
WHEN THE WANDERERS COME HOME
UNIVERSITY OF NEBRASKA PRESS, 2016

Our people say, "The wandering child does not know its mother's grave."
—GREBO (AFRICAN) PROVERB

So I Stand Here

They say thresholds are meant to keep

the outsider out, the insider, in. Crickets
forever, creeping along walls, along the edges

of things. You must first lift your right foot,
and then the left, and then enter the hut

before the kola nut is served, before
the spiced pepper is offered, and the water

from the stream, handed to you. This is
the way of things, the way of life, clay to clay,

your hand holds not just a cup of water,
but the source of life. Tradition. After that,

the outsider is now an insider, but everywhere
I go, my country people have become

a different people. So, I stand here,
an outsider, at the doorpost. Do not tell me

that these corrugated old dusty roads
have emerged of themselves out of the war.

Or that the new songs these strangers sing
in this now strange country of ours, are

from the time before the bullets. Do not tell
me that the kola nut you served me

will answer all of the questions that linger
in my soul. Do not tell me that I belong

to this new people. I have wandered away
too long, my kinsmen. I have wandered so far,

my feet no longer know how to walk the old
paths we used to walk. I do not know these

people, birthed from the night's passing
of lost ghosts. I do not know these people

who have so sadly emerged out of the womb
of war after the termite's feasting.

My kola nut has lost its taste, and the spiced
pepper, now, with a new spice. I am too

impure to meet my ancestors, and the gourd
of water I have just fetched from *Nganlun*

weighs heavily upon my head. I stand
at the threshold, my kinsmen, come and help

me over the doorpost that the termites
have eaten. I do not have the hands to greet

my ancestors. I do not have the hands
to greet my kinswomen, and the hand with

which I take hold of the kola nut is shriveled
by travel. The kola nut you served me

is no longer bitter, oh come, my kinswomen,
the horn blower has lost his voice. But they

tell me that the horn blower does not need
his voice to blow the horn to let me in.

The Cities We Lost

After they left, rainy days came back
to find us
            among the ruins, in a city
resting on crutches.

There were the cliffs as if falling.

Old cliffs, old town, old villages,
the far wanderer, even the birds would
not stop looking.

The forgotten bones came alive, rising
on wings and black wandering feet,

then came looking,
            for those taken from among us,
for those of us left to fade into air.
On the road,

            a child was looking, sharp jaw
bones, tiny hands,
no need for crutches. The child had
become her own crutches of thin legs,
            no voice to carry away her legs,
no tears to open up her eyes to the sun,
as if she no longer needed voice.

But she thought I was her mother,
at the roadside.
            Maybe I was her mother,

sitting there, by the roadside.
And looking up at me
as if to follow this stranger that I was,
but how could I claim her

in the ruins that we had become?
            Amidst the bullets and rebels,
the suffocation of death
            and the dying,
death was more alive than us.

What Took Us to War

Every so often, you find
a piece of furniture, an old head wrap
or something like a skirt
held together by a rusty pin.
Our years, spilled all over the ruggedness
of this war-torn place,
our years, wasted like grains of rice.

Relics of your past, left for you,
in case you returned accidentally
or intentionally, in case you did not
perish with everyone else.
Something hanging onto thread,
holding onto the years
to be picked up, after locusts
and termites have had their say,
the graciousness of looters,

the graciousness of termites
and temporary owners of a home
you built during your youth,
during the Samuel Doe years
when finding food was your life goal.
How gracious, the war years,
how gracious, the warlords,
their fiery tongues and missiles.

All the massacres we denied,
and here we are today, coming upon
a woodwork of pieces of decayed
people that are not really pieces
of woodwork at all.
This should be an antique, a piece
of the past that refused to die.

Wood does not easily rot, but here,
termites have taken over Congo Town
the way Charles Taylor claimed the place,
the way Charles Taylor claimed
our land and the hearts of hurting people,
the way the Atlantic in its wild roaming
has eaten its way into town
even as we roamed, in search of refuge,

the way whole buildings have crumbled
into the sea, the way the years
have collapsed upon years.
What took us to war has again begun,
and what took us to war
has opened its wide mouth
again to confuse us.
What took us to war, oh, my people!

I NEED TWO BODIES

One, to sleep and the other
to shuffle, push and grind up the day.
One, to bend a rod,
and set the world upright,
the other, to cuddle the earth
so it holds on to its hold.

One, to inhale and the other, to exhale.
One, to lie down upon freshly dewed grass,
the orange red sun, dying down slowly
in my other body's eye.

I want my other body to drive like
a stubborn engine as stubborn
as a woman, after middle age,
my other body, standing on metal legs,
ready to grind
a large day downhill.
To empty these muscles of aching
pains down some drain.

I want my working body to sigh
and stand firm to all the battles
a woman must wage
against the grind of unsuspecting
roadblocks. One body, to be

the everlasting pull against push,
my one body, unbridled; legs,
as concrete as the Statue of Liberty
on a cloudy morning,
her gazing eyes upon
my old tired face as I sit
on a far ferry into the city
quiet, as sleep.

Then, my sleeping, eating,
resting body, rising out of unnecessary
things, tells this old one, "Be still,
be still and know that I am you.
Be still, and know
that I am Woman."

THE CREATION

Woman was made so clothes would have something
to wear. So shoes would find company, hair,

finely braided, hanging down the shoulders of an
unloose woman. A tightly fitted skirt, finding knees.

Some *lappa* suit, carved out of unyielding things.
Stiff fingers, sewing and sewing, until fabric

attaches itself to permanent skin. All the lost hours
and lost sleep, just so fabric can find sliding ground

on the back of a woman, feeding herself on scraps
of unwanted love in a city, long-lost to map builders.

Woman was made so pavement would have feet
to carry. Loads of sharp heels, bare, only to shoes.

So feet would know the forgetfulness that comes
with stepping, the forgetfulness of twisting not just

to the rhythm of new love. Woman was made
so men would have trouble to fall into. Like a ditch,

dug so deep, falling into it only creates deep scars
in an already scarred heart. Woman was made

so worry would have a place to lease, so the sun
would find moon, so moon would have daylight

to blame for its own disappearance, so worry
would burn down the throat of some lonely man.

Woman was made to put the world in places where
place cannot hold earth. Woman, carved crudely

out of the beauty of ugliness, out of scarred pieces
of pain. Beauty, out of all the broken parts of a broken

city, where the heart has forgotten how to mend.
Woman was built out of corrugated pieces of zinc,

just so the earth would rebuild, so pain would forget
how to be. Earth, finding erectness in the small,

bent, carved places, where the world has been so
long broken, there is no longer any unmaking.

Woman was made to remake other women into
other hard pieces of burnt clay. So the clothing

we wear could talk to other clothing we can't wear.
Woman was made from scarred tissues of metal,

from the firmness of a brick wall, iron pieces
standing up at last for something. So tears

would have a face to wear, so pain would have
something to carry around, so the earth would

find the heart to heal all the brokenness of ruin.
Woman was made to unmake a man the way

you unmake a face the way you undo, to rewind
the corrugated heart of a world, too long broken.

BECOMING GHOST

for the women telling me their war stories

My friends tell me that every photo I take
is a different person. As if each individual pose,

every bit of every effort by a photographer
has refused to see the same person twice.

As if a changing person were inside the single
person, as if I were a new personality of itself

outside of itself each time. So I stare at photos
taken at the same moment, same poses, same

suit, same red-framed glasses against jawline.
I sit still to see how the same woman can occupy

so many spaces and spirits, power to power,
spirit against spirit, as if an outside spirit were

to inhabit her being. As if I have been taken over
by many wailing women on their way to their

executions, on their way to mutilation, the power
of rape, so powerless. And the execution

of women, which, in itself leaves the war-ravished
warrior mutilated inside out, the emptiness

of ruined spaces, where a rebel never knows
when to end rebellion. As if I were being occupied

by the empty arms of those women, led away
from us, in line, their screaming infants, tossed

aside like dirt, or dashed against a wall that
knows not how to swallow blood, being asked

to swallow blood, the untold stories of unknown
women, walking, barefoot, drowned, after rape.

As if rape were not in itself an abomination.
I have become all the stories I've jammed into

the small spaces of a digital world of flash cards
and drives, too minute to hold up history

in its flat brain. A woman, half seated on a chair,
staring into the small space of my camcorder

lens, as if afraid of both the camera and the story
she will empty into the camcorder. As if, afraid

to own the chair and the story being held up
by the four frail legs of the chair. It is 2011,

and I'm still collecting Liberian women's war
stories that otherwise are dying. The victim, who

dies twice with the story, dying a hundred times.
As if I were the mind of many ghosts, collecting

ghost stories, the mind that discovers more bones
at the burial site of old human skulls and bones,

we came here to forget. The room, full of women
who have come like an army of women to tell their

stories, are in tears now. I leave the room so they
do not see my own tears. There will never be

tissues sufficient to drown the cries of so many ills.
The woman stares into my camcorder as I return

to stand beside her while the camcorder rolls
in the hands of my assistant at the other end.

This camcorder may now know how to wail
silently in each telling. And then, the woman

drops her own bomb just like all the other women.
Oh, how each one of us carries between our

breasts, stories no one will believe. You can never
be the same after this sort of story-collecting

session, I tell you. To ask a woman to hold down
the legs of her younger brother, to hold him

in place, to calm his fighting legs and body
as rebels shave off his head is to ask her to die

forever inside out. Is to ask her to move her body
inside the body of another woman, is to ask her

to live a life of dying again and again. To ask her
to hold down her mother's last son, the same legs

she held, to change his diapers, her mother, looking
on, so long ago to see how a girl becomes woman,

not knowing there was a future somewhere, so
heartless, where her girl-child would become

woman through rape, through an abomination
of the sort that kills a nation, where sacrifice asks

too much of the sacrificial lamb. I am inhabiting
so many women's bodies. I am inhabiting living

ghosts, my people. I am becoming a body of water
as if my own tears were not sufficient for my one life.

As if all the tears of this nation could purify a land
so stained, it has become too impure for redemption.

As if this body of mine were sufficient in itself
to carry my own near-death stories, as if I have

become a new ghost, occupied by many other ghosts.
As if I have stopped being so the dead will live.

When Monrovia Rises

The city is not a crippled woman at all. This city
is not a blind man at a potholed roadside, his

cane, longer than his eye, waiting for coins to fall
into his bowl, in a land where all the coins were lost

at war. When Monrovia rises, the city rises with
a bang, and I, throwing off my damp beddings,

wake up with a soft prayer on my lips. Even God
in the Heavens knows how fragile this place is.

This city is not an egg or it would have long
emerged from its shell, a small fiery woman

with the legs of snakes. All day, boys, younger
than history can remember, shout at one another

on a street corner near me about a country they
have never seen. Girls wearing old T-shirts speak

a new language, a corruption by that same ugly war.
You see, they have never seen better times.

Everyone here barricades themselves behind steel
doors, steel bars, and those who can afford also

have walls this high. Here, we're all afraid that one
of us may light a match and start the fire again

or maybe one among us may break into our home
and slash us all up not for our wealth, but for

the memories they still carry under angry eyelids.
Maybe God will come down one day without his boots.

Maybe someone will someday convince us that after
all the city was leveled, we are all the same after all,

same mother, same father, same root, same country,
all of us, branches and limbs of the same oak.

This Is the Real Leaving

This is the real leaving, and as I look around
this Pagos Island neighborhood, where we

used to think the world held its poles together
around us, I'm afraid of saying goodbye.

Here, the neighbor children cling and cling, their
eyes, uncertain of tomorrow. But children do not

always know that they are poor or wretched,
and cannot discern how their future will be

by what they eat or wear. They cannot
always see into tomorrow from where they live

or what degree of poverty they possess, or the
difference between what their neighbors own,

nor can they know how wealthy others are
by the material possessions, scattered around

a neighbor's yard. Maybe they wonder why.
Maybe they do not wonder. I walked in the door

yesterday, and emptied a fridge full of *torborgee*,
palm butter, fried fish and so much good food

my son had left uneaten. They may never know
why I'm angry that there's food in my fridge

while others starve; today, the neighborhood
children had a feast; one feast, one big meal

today, but tomorrow, there will be nothing.
This is the real leaving, the detachment from

clinging things and people, and so often, I am so
broken, I become like a hard string, an angry

thing, baffled by this unevenness of a world
we are able to change. I wake up, and in my heart,

I am holding onto a child whose mother's protruding
abdomen was so alive, but today, upon my return,

they tell me the child died soon after birth, an
infant, born, already lacking blood, born in a shack.

How does the world expect an infant whose mother
has no blood to bring forth a child with blood

in its veins? This is the real leaving, a departure
from clinging things, forever imbedded in my heart.

To recover a world once lost is as hard as crossing
the stream of swampland between Paynesville

and me, the swamp behind my yard, the swampland
between the place where poverty ends and where

wealth begins. This is the real leaving, my child,
this is where we leave the shores to paddle afar,

but in paddling, we lose the shores, where we were
born to wade the deep waters our mothers could

not wade. And yet, in wading, we have to leave again.

In My Dream

In my dream, I'm on the road, flying
somewhere, stranded at an airport.
I've lost my car or lost the keys
in my lost purse.
Or I'm in the airport security line
without my passport, a lone traveler
without a country.

So they want to know my country.
They want to know my place of birth.
They want to know the map that got me lost.
They want to know the name of those
who shattered my dream,
shattered my lost country.

So I say, I'm a woman looking for home,
displaced, a bag of useless goods
for my journey, a flip-flap, a ragged
bundle that only a refugee carries.
I'm the lost and unfound, from those
who did not come on boats,

those that did not come ticketed
in chains, those who did not fit in chains,
those, neither welcome by those who came
on boats nor in chains. I'm among
the newcomers, the new, newcomers.
Those who came, ticketed

not by plane tickets or train tickets.
Those who came ticketed by live bullets,
grenades and rocket missiles,
those, still bleeding from their sides,
those who found their way here
by crawling among the dead.

I WANT TO BE THE WOMAN

I don't want to be the other woman.
Don't want to stay up nights
for the phone call.
Take your excuses and pour them
down some rusty drain
as from a wine bottle,
and kill yourself at dawn.

I want to stay the woman who stands
there, waiting,
so her husband's lies rest like dust
on the windshield of an old car.
I want to carry deep scars
of brokenness all my life,
like our mothers' mothers' mothers,
who did not learn how to kill
that old African polygamy,
but killed it anyway.

I am The Woman, the maker of the bed,
the unused love keeper, the breeder
of fine children, scarred
only by broken dreams in the broken places,
where our foremothers found company
with other women, and buried
their babies' naval strings with hopes
that someday, something would happen.
No, I am already The Woman,
Khade-Wheh, headwife,
the home-keeper, *Khade*, the owner
of the afterbirth and the afterbirth pains,

Khade-Wheh, the holder of hot pots,
the keeper of the homestead,
the fireplace holder,
the powerless, powerful African woman,
after the old paths
of lonely women, betrothed
too early to unknown, ugly men.
No, I am not looking for love.

This body is too old
for lovers to hang out in my dreams
or in my daydreaming.

Don't lie to me. I am too beautiful for you.
Don't fool yourself. I do not need love.
I do not think my *Iyeeh* knew love,
and I used to hear her say
that love could not make a farm.
My *Iyeeh*, whose bare feet
grew thorns from walking back
and forth from farm to farm homestead,
from farm to town, from tilling the land
like a husbandless wife,

my *Iyeeh*, who entertained all
the small wives of an already blind husband,
my *Bai*, who was not too blind
to sleep with multiple wives,
but *Iyeeh* had only one husband despite
the crowd of wives
populating her marriage.
Yes, I want to be the villain
only to my husband. I want to ground
my last years under a cold blanket,
to guard my woman part
from your invasion.
I want to greet my ancestors, our mothers,
with this old piece of my brokenness.
Yes, I am *Khade-Wheh*,
the mother of mothers.

A Room with a View

From my hospital room window, the city rises
through sky, steel city, three rivers, bridges,

broken and unbroken. A friend once told me
how this city has more bridges than any other

city, bridges so broken, they have become only
relics of the past. Outside my window, an old,

old city theater, where students from grade
schools stand in line for a visit, but my camera

lens is only for the homes on the far hill; homes,
I have heard to come down, sliding when heavy

rains overwhelm the city, but again, they rise,
like towers, and their owners again repossess them.

This third day, fifth round of chemotherapy opens
slowly with rain, fog, clouds, so the windowpanes

in my photo remind me that even a rainy day can
be beautiful as the beauty of hard times, the beauty

in the mystery of illness, the quiet of a hospital
room, when all you can do is reflect on the beauty

of your past life through raindrops against your
window glass, the beauty of homes against

the distant hills, bridge upon bridge, and the warmth
of my beddings, reminding me that I am still here.

Losing Hair

It's June 9, my sister Nanu's birthday,
and I am losing my hair.

The girl from Tugbakeh with all that hair,
her body so full of hair, hair down her

shoulders, hair, almost shutting her eyelids,
the girl that could have made a living selling

hair strands, now losing it all to the poisonous
venom of chemotherapy.

To keep life in my veins, they must purge
all life out of my veins. Life for life, hair

strand for hair strand, all the cells of my
body, crying out "don't kill me," but dying

still, so killer cells can drown themselves
in the war for life. I feel like I'm again at war,

Liberia, in a refugee camp, where Peace Keepers
cannot keep peace without war, cannot save life

without the taking of life. To rescue us, they
shoot and kill, and all around, we lie dead.

The cells of my fine body, all dying, and if
there is a resurrection of dead cells, my cells

will again rise out of nothing, and all these
black strands of hair now falling with the gray

will know the solitude of losing, the solitude
of the survival's story, the solitude of cancer,

will know the absoluteness of fighting cancer.

Hair

So your hair has decided to leave you.
Be calm, this is a sacred moment.
So you're standing before the mirror,
horrified. Loads of long strands
have curled themselves for departure
from your head.
Soon, you will be as bald as a glass wall,
as bare as sidewalk, as a clay pot,
as jar, as marble, as solid as a globe,
your baldness, balder than bald,
but you are still a woman.
The despair they said you would know
has also left you.
After all, who needs hair
if they cannot live life?
After all, what is hair to a dead person
in a casket? After all,
how does the grave reconcile itself
to your long, dark hair
if not losing hair were a death sentence?
So, like the silly child that you are,
though grown and aging, a woman
after menopause, who under attack
by cancer, refuses to fall,
dance. Dance your way into life
again, into the beauty of the years
to come, into the days when your
grandchildren arrive to greet you,
dance with laughter, after all the pain
of chemo, the pain of hair
falling at your feet on your bathroom floor,
dance and make music come to life.
You will live through this.
And afterward, you will forget
you were even woman enough
to wonder about hair.
Dance and laugh, and let it fall.
Unless a seed falls to the ground and dies,
it cannot come to life, you were told.
So, dance into the new hair
that awaits you some day.

2014, My Mama Never Knew You

When 2014 came in, we saw fireworks.
We saw wineglasses. We saw what we
always see on that first dark morning.
That life would be as kind to us as July rain,
as gentle as dew.
We saw a road that did not lead uphill
among gravel and thorns. We saw beauty,
the coming of spring and the birds,
flowers in bloom, not only on the branches
of trees, but in our eyes.
I saw it all, sitting on my living room
carpet, counting down.

I did not know that the year's counting down
was counting down for real.
Barely the year was in, and here came news
that somewhere inside my womb
was not a baby, was not fibroids, was not
anything you could just go in and slash out,
but inside that tender place, where only
warmth and love used to hold my babies
in place for nine months, in that beloved
and holy space was something as strange
as nothing my mother could have known.
So, when the doctor said "cancer,"
I thought she'd had too many wines.

So, like the warrior woman I was made to be,
I rose, upright, the way a farmer woman
grabs her hoe and her other tools around her
to capture the horrors of farming,
the way a newly widowed girl
calculates the farm work only she must do.
I stood up, and went to war
with this old Monster that has known only
strength over the decades at war with my fellow
women warriors. I went to battle,
only my heart as tool, only my strength, only
my bare fingers, my sense of humor and my soul.

Somehow, I said to myself,
that if a woman can walk among the dead in one
of the world's bloodiest civil wars,
that same woman can meet and conquer
the Monster. I did not raise my white flag,
seeking to make peace with the Monster.
I did not lie down to die nor did I lay my tools down.
I went to war, the way all women have gone
to war bringing to life all the human
creatures earth has ever known.

After the womb was pulled out of place, its screws
uprooted and its loose parts, counted, the chain
that keeps life in place, unchained,
I cradled my face in my palms and wept hard,
that weeping a woman does when a child
is yanked out of her by nature.
So, I thought, well, it is all over now.
2014, I now saw the walls of my heart coming
back in place, as if the heart's walls could
of their own, fall and rise of their own.

Then comes May, flowers, here in my yard,
cool, misty winds, birds, returning
to present themselves, birds, affirming that
indeed, we can die and be rebirthed, May,
and I was now home, my womb, happily gone
and with no regrets, since a woman
who has already given her seeds
to the world in four living children, has no
need to wail over departed wombs and tubes,
and all that comes with the territory.
I met May, bruised, but alive, me, alive,
after the knife, after the scare of not waking up,
I held out my hand for May.

But somehow, in between the pain and the hope,
my father died. 2014, the year my mother
should have warned me about.
May, my father lay dead in a cold mortuary

in a faraway country that is not a faraway
country at all; my father, gone, and here I am,
fighting the Monster. Now, there was chemotherapy
at my door, and death news arrived on my phone
in a store parking lot, me, imprisoned,
not only in a car, but so far from that first

Po-po-wlee call, the coming of the *Nehwordeh*,
our townswomen, the daughters of the clan,
the gathering of the clan to open the door
so my father would cross over the threshold
into the other world.
I was not there when they laid *The Mat* down.

I like to take my days on pieces of splintered
wood. I like to take my life on slow ground,
when not just tears can heal my heart:

But it is only seven months, and now,
a new monster, Ebola, like war, like cancer,
they call it Ebola, a plague, the untouchables
are the dying, but doctors and nurses die first.
How much death does it take for God to wake
up an evil people? How many plagues?
Why does a flower rise out of a petal at dawn
just to die before it unfolds itself?
Sometimes, I want to just walk until I walk
until I walk to a place where I was meant to go.
Sometimes, the road itself loses its footpath.
Sometimes, all we can do is to stand here
and fight the Monster.
Sometimes, I start my day with a prayer.
Maybe, this is all I was born to do.

III

Poems from:
WHERE THE ROAD TURNS
AUTUMN HOUSE PRESS, 2010

"We departed our homelands, and we came."
—GREBO SAYING (LIBERIAN)

IN THE BEGINNING II

In the beginning,
God took clay
and he took rocks
and he took a green, slimy leaf
and he made man.

He took a twig from afar
and twisted the twig between
his bare fingers
and he turned the twig
into a woman.

Then God took the sun
and he took the moon
and he took the earth
and placed them all
on a flat plate.

Then he called the woman
and the man, and in the presence
of the man and the woman
he took the plate,
holding the moon

and the sun and the earth,
and handed them all to the woman.
She looked at God, and she
wondered. The woman
looked at God,
and smiled.

Then the woman walked away
with the sun and the moon
and the earth
while the man wondered
for some time about
what his eyes had seen.

It came to pass
that the man began to fight
to take from the woman, the sun
and the moon and the earth
that God had given.

Then the man fought and fought
until he broke down all the bridges
and the skyscrapers, the satellites
and the towers
that they had built.

And the woman stood in wonder
as all around them,
the man tore down everything
that God had created,

everything that she had brought
forth. And with his hands,
the man tore down
everything around them,
and after that,
there was nothing.

Biography When the Wanderers Come Home

This is where we were born,
in these corrugated rugged places,
where boys chasing girls chasing
boys chasing other girls chasing bellies
chasing babies chasing other babies
chasing poverty, chased death.
Of potholed streets and bars and sex
and other girls, getting drowned
forever and ever in loveless love.
And then the fires of our lives
lit other fires of other lives
with lust and then
there was no longer us.
So then the war came with its bullets,
chasing people chasing the bombs,
and ghost towns sprang up
with carcasses of the dying
and the dead. And like mushrooms,
the dead rose up to claim the land
and we were no more.
But the fires still burned in the wombs
and in the eyes of the city streets
below which the dead lovers and
love lie. And there was life again
out of so much pain,
and life took on its own life again
and the girls returned on the backs
of surreal horses in search
of that old fire. But these were no longer
the same girls or boys or men or women.
But this is where we grew up, on these
sidewalk streets, in these rugged places.
This is where the streets come in.
This is where we belong.
This is where life begins.

Love Song before the Sun Goes Down

I'm afraid of losing you, Titi, my love.
Your laughing eyes, now so cold
even when the gap of your front teeth
still tingles my heart while you grow cold.
When the sun goes down
on my hut, and there are no more children
singing under the moonlight,
and the village boys come out with their
sleeping eyes, Titi, do not let your heart
wander away from me-oh.

I grow old, Titi, I grow old, but my love
for you, Titi, my love sits fresh
like pebbles in the stream where the lover
escaping his lover's flames
was drowned in a stream so shallow,
but the lover, escaping the flames
of his lover was still drowned,
face down; he was found lying face down,
Titi, my beautiful dark-skinned bride.

Is it not youth that you seek, Titi, my bride?
Is it not the horn blower that you want, Titi?
I am still the horn blower who fell for you
at the onset of not just your youth.
I am still the horn blower that you loved
with the love of fresh dew drops.
Do not let the fire grow dim, Titi, my love.
Do not let the timbers burn themselves
out on this old love, Titi, oh Titi,
my beautiful long-haired bride.

FOR MY HUSBAND AFTER SO MANY YEARS
for Mlen-Too

So this is the bed. So this is the life
of the after-years of the years after.
The candlelight lingers late after all these years.
Someone is watching us.
This journey has been long, so if there are roses
bring them to me in a tall vase.
Carnations don't do me good, and hibiscus
that I miss so much don't do well in a vase.
Come, sit beside me like a new lover.
Like a lover, seeking to make new the years
we've held together between so many wars
and so many teardrops, so many laughs and lives.
It is as if we are other people from other lives,
as if we have lived and lived for others
who never knew how to live, as if this fire,
I say this fire, my lover, husband, my lover,
husband, the father of my children, the father
of the children I never had, the father
of the children who returned
because they hated my womb.
Sometimes, my womb weeps for them;
sometimes, my womb dances.
Maybe my womb was insufficient
for the fire they carried from the other world.
Oh, my lover, my husband of so many years
I cannot count. So, what was it you said
when you recalled how after all these years,
here we are, all the other lovers lost at sea,
and here we are, beside the fireplace, the fire,
so soft. The children are growing old on us now,
my darling, come, this is me.
Do not linger too late.
I was made just for this time and you, for me.
We grow old. We grow old.
Can you put the fire out now?

So This Is Where the Roads Merge
a poem for Sister Agnes

So this is where the water must go—gravel, silt and all?
Where the sinkhole sinks, where the ground goes
underground, where love descends under the goalkeeper
of the dream, where the dream must finally evolve?

So this is the flooding ground, the protector now staring
wide-eyed at love in its final hour, where a woman
may fall down her own cliff. Another marriage, ending
after the palm wine was spilled and not spilled.
It is my girlfriend from Michigan on the phone, my

Liberian sister-friend who married her sweetheart
from her dream world, the college boyfriend every
girl wanted for a husband. So this is where the roads
must merge, in the developer's manhole, in the
sinking valley? Out here in Pennsylvania, the hills merge

into more hills, where the walker must first see the hills
from down below, the slow climb that reminds one
of child-birthing, pushing and pushing until
the child's head emerges into a world, where everything
can depend on what happens at the crossroads.

I'm writing a poem for you, Agnes, on my long walk.
In my neighborhood, builders are digging
so new gravel can sink. Agnes,
the once happy-wife-housekeeper
of more than thirty years, the warrior, sister-woman.

So this is where a woman empties her years
into the sinkhole, her years of cooking and washing
and cleaning, years of babies and the after-babies,
of in-law evenings and prepared smiles during cocktail
nights, the woman-made-husband now, taller

than the creator of his dream, his goalkeeper, now down,
after her milk was sapped dry, the warrior woman's
husband, now, another woman's husband,
where the road must end, and the calabash, broken.
So this is what our mothers did not tell us?

A Memorial for Herb Scott: One Year Later
February 12, 2007

I want to remember you just the way you were.
A man, almost too tall for life,
standing at my door in Kalamazoo,
that small bend as if to apologize for your height.
I flipped open my front door, and there you were
in search of more poetry the way a hunter
follows deer tracks through snow country,
through wooded tracks,
through an alleyway of unfamiliar woods.

The poem I'm writing for you will be choppy
and stale, unedited and spent.
Time for freshness passed away with your leaving.
I used to watch you on an office chair, the sun
looking on, and I'd be there,
my manuscript under your sharp eyes;
you, holding on to a line of one of my poems,
dangling it before me and asking,
"Is this you? Is this your voice?"

I'd be there, sometimes, standing suddenly,
battling to save some useless image in my lines,
to save some figure of speech not so ready to let go.
I'd be there, hiding my fear of losing a word or two.
Afraid I'd have to rewrite an entire book of poems.
Afraid I'd have to redo my bullet-shelled streets,
redo Monrovia, redo a child soldier
and his weapon, shortened just for him.

Maybe I'd have to redo the faces of the women
who scarred the stories inside my poems,
redo the silences I grew to create and recreate,
take Monrovia to task again so anyone
reading me would not see my tears without seeing
the scarred pieces of people and their cry
that was too inaudible for pain.
So a reader can lift my lines to a burning flame,
examine them, hold them,
and let them float through wind and sky.

Standing there beside you, I'd say,
"Yes, Herb, that's my voice, don't you hear it?"
Your head, balding at queer places, and your fingers,
struggling to hold on to the pen, coming down
on a word, your pen that had drawn all sorts of lines
through my manuscripts, and I'd stare at you
aging, but not truly aging,
and I'd say to myself, "Boy!"

Scared of losing you, of losing your twists
and turns on the chair as you examined my poems
as if you were god of the word, god of the line,
father of the image, father of the painter of the image.
Then I'd think to myself, *God, he's already dying,*
this man, already dying.
The big sun, coming through your office window,
and I thought, *everyone I know is dying*
all the time; dying or getting ready to die
or planning to die.

We'd fight, you and I, over my African repetitions,
my syntax and tone, and you'd smile,
"It's great, this one is great, and this is you;
that's your voice, but this one, it's some
other girl down the road somewhere; get it out."

One day, you wanted to know why these women
"sitting on *The Mat*," wailed for two weeks in my poem,
and I said, "That's culture, Grebo people,
Grebo funerals, Grebo rituals."
So you said, "Well, I can understand this repetition now.
Any time a group of people can sit on a mat,
mourning for two weeks, they've got to run
out of new words sooner or later."

A Lover Lost at Sea

Sometimes, I am that woman whose lover
was abandoned at sea.
After the ship was wrecked,
after the divers were brought in by boats
and after diving and diving again and again,
after the foaming waves rose and settled,
after the onlookers and the grieving family
were held up at bay, waiting and waiting,
and then one day, the search is over.
That last wringing of search tools,
that last wiping of sandy feet,
the divers, departing, and up above,
the sun also sets.
I am that woman, sometimes,
whose husband takes a pot of unearned
love and pours it into a drain,
whose husband pulls down
all the world's forgiveness on himself.
I am that woman, I say, I am that woman,
barefoot upon the hot sand, waiting
for a lover, lost at sea, waiting
for a lover, long-lost at sea.

ONE DAY

love song for the newly divorced

One day, you will awake from your covering
and that heart of yours will be totally mended,
and there will be no more burning within.
The owl, calling in the setting of the sun
and the deer path, all erased.
And there will be no more need for love
or lovers or fears of losing lovers
and there will be no more burning timbers
with which to light a new fire,
and there will be no more husbands or people
related to husbands, and there will be no more
tears or reason to shed your tears.
You will be as mended as the bridge
the working crew have just reopened.
The thick air will be vanquished with the tide
and the river that was corrupted by lies
will be cleansed totally and free.
And the rooster will call in the setting sun
and the sun will beckon homeward,
hiding behind your one tree that was not felled.

Ghosts Don't Go Away Just Like That

Sometimes they lurk in hallways where they have lost
the other side of them. They may hover over new wars,

like the wars that carried them away from their bodies,
causing them to lose their world and us in the rush.

Ghosts don't go away just like that, you know;
they may come in that same huge crowd that was

massacred together with them, and since that massacre
may have happened at school, in a bar or at church, they

may be found, kneeling at the pulpit, singing and taking
communion again and again, with everyone else.

They gather on a Saturday evening, as the sun sets over
the hills and a small flash of yesterday's lightning lingers

from that old storm as the new storm rides in, and then,
there they are, ghosts! You can see them only if you have

eyes to see them as ghosts of humans, and yet not ghosts.
They're looking to see if we will recall that they were here.

To see if we will build a stone to honor the fact that they
were here, with us, walking and talking, like us, to see

if we will remember that they lost so much blood
in the shooting, that they broke a leg or two, and that

so many of them were not counted in that sad number.
They want to know if we will put up a stone or keep

the fire burning to put out the fires, to stop all the killing
in the city streets around the world,

to stop all the killing in the eyes of the city streets.

WHERE THE ROAD TURNS

I'm right here on the road, in the open.
You will find me waiting where Gbarnga's
hills curve into zigzags, and cars slow down
because potholes have taken over the road,
because potholes have taken over my life.
Where on school days, rich children
used to carry bookbags halfway
in their arms, kicking stones on the ground
or counting stones, or maybe not counting
or kicking anything but air. Today, potholes
have settled air in places. You will find me
in the corner, where the street forgot to pass,
where my little shack sits here, being
forgotten, and muddy puddles slowly
become river, winding away. Every car will
splash muddy water in your face if you stand
here, waiting. I still wait here,
in the corner road, cutting, weeding,
watering already sun burnt plants, waiting
because someone told me that if I could
wait long enough, just long enough, things
will change; the government will change;
food will come for us refugees,
something will happen for my good.
That I, who used to feed my neighbors,
should now wait days, weeks, months on a dying
roadside for free food that never comes,
that may never come until I, too, am dead.

We Departed Our Homelands and We Came
Grebo Saying

We departed our homelands and we came,
so the Grebo say, we came with our hands
and we came with our machetes

so we too, could carve up the new land.

When we left home, we crossed streams
and we climbed up hills; we set out through
wet brushes, and the rivers parted
so we could cross.

We know that if the leopard should leap,
it is because it sees an antelope passing.

We came, not so we could sit and watch
a wrestling match, not so we could watch
the land on which our feet walk,
rise beyond our reach.

*We journeyed from our homelands,
and we came,* so let it be known, *that we left
our homelands, and we came.*

When we arrived, we dug up the earth,
and in this new earth, we laid down
our umbilical cords, forever.

So let it be known among the people, *we left
all the beauty of our homelands,* not so

we would sit out on *The Mat* to wail.

THE PEOPLE WALKING IN DARKNESS

a song for Barack Obama:
November 4, 2008

Put the music on, I say, put the music on, the people
walking in darkness have seen a great light.

Let drums sound loud in the hill country, in the desert
country, on dry roads and muddy roads.

Let the earth be still, the souls of our ancestors are
passing. Let the earth be still, the souls of our ancestors

are passing. May the dancing girls come out, tapping their
feet lightly to *Wayee* and to *Sumu*, and let the young men

beating our drums sing no longer with mournful cries.
Let those women singing their dirges, be comforted, I say.

Let young boys in the village square hold on to their
lovers, ah, the *Town Crier* now sings an ancient song.

So, let the drums pound, I say *Klan-klan-teh*, Obama
has prevailed over his foes, oh Africa, the lion has

sprinted ahead of his pursuers. May the trumpeters
come out, sweating with music. And may the earth know

the silence of the jungles, I say, may our eyes take hold
of this day that has broken over the fields, oh, my people,

the day has broken over the fields-oh. Our wandering
children will once more find their footing from

this wandering. On the road, a farmer stands no longer
in mid-road. So come, and let us hold up the fire

so lightning can pass, so our children can pass, so lovers
can come out of hiding. Let daylight break out

upon the hills, so our ancestors who lost their footing
at the hands of Slavery will shake loose grave dirt in their

unmarked graves. Obama, the son of a woman, the one
son we were all going to bring forth has become ours.

Bring the kola nuts and spiced pepper, and let
libation cleanse these parched surfaces where the earth

has long been bleeding. The child that was left behind
has cleared the path so our feet can find new footing.

The stone that was abandoned has become our resting
place, so, our wailing can end, so, our children can live,

so we can step over the threshold, where we have so long
waited in the dark rainy night. Finally, here we are today,

the once untouchable stool has become ours, oh my father!
The people walking in darkness have seen a great light,

I say, the people long left in darkness have seen a great light.

SOME THINGS YOU NEVER STOP LOOKING FOR

Your mother's last words before she was ready to go,
those moments of lost days, your last image

of her that had nothing to do with dying.
That too, lost to memory or memory to the image.

Then there's the memory card where on a photo,
you waved and waved at moments on their way
to being lost, where the photographer

was your last crush before you walked up or down
the aisles with someone else, and the crush,
standing on the sidewalk
as your wedding procession rolled by.

Then there are those moments when you almost
lost it on the birthing table; blood and water,

rushing out with the baby, the dirty water being
spilled in the baby's eyes, and now, someone has
to save your last born from drowning
in her own water rescue.

But over and over, you lost the hope of seeing it all,
of seeing the bleeding, the stitching and the rush

to save you from drowning yourself in that sacred
moment. That first shrill cry of your own baby,
and the finality of innocence.

But you've never stopped looking for your sweet
cousin who died in this same universal chamber, one

life for one life, your cousin Hazel, gone just like that.
Someone told you later that the afterbirth can refuse

to let go of its owner, but when the life that was birthed
became lost too, after the burial and the wailing, after

the mute line of handshakes, the child, also lost,
you've never stopped searching for the reason why.

All the cherished spaces you gave up at adolescence
just so you would become.
How your own heart was broken over and over

until you grew up to discover that the heart cannot
become steel unless it is broken over and over.

So you seek out the steel, and with a slice of steel
from your heart, you mend your own heart.

After that, you discovered how sweet it is for the heart
to be broken just so you can carry something
with a scar on your person.

But you've never stopped looking for those lost places
of childhood, your father's house, where the river's flow
had nothing to do with the river's flow.

And here you are, still seeking solitudes, searching
for friends you lost growing up, for friends you
lost, fleeing, for the friends you never had,

for the friends you will never meet on this side of life,
lost lovers, lost kisses and hugs and the tears
              when you were only seventeen.

What about your crush on your favorite teacher
who couldn't even remember your name?

All of this to arrive here, still searching for a lost sock
here, a lost boot there, a child's glove, even though
              the child now stands taller than you.

There are those things you forever seek, the lost disk,
with your entire life story jammed into it,
and the loss in your sweetheart's eyes,

where the landscape stretches so wide,
              even the eye loses ground looking.

Coming Home
a song for the war returnees

After the rain, that first sunshine, like
a new lover, and it seems the world

    has just begun all over again.

From the hill,
                I used to crop my knees
at my backdoor stairway
    to watch the mist ride

above the swamps or the swamps above
the river or the poverty of the people

above the thieves, robbing us of this land.

In the city, the whole world has sent
its messengers
    to help the newly rich eat up the land
    from beneath our feet.

They say the war is over, but the poor still groan.
The land groans. From the earth,
    hot mist rises out of bloody ground,
out of landfills of carcasses of the war,
and the people
    in their forever poverty,

return from war, where some of them
have left their legs and arms and hearts and hope.

The people have returned,
             poorer than the red ant.

STEP LIGHTLY, GOD: A MEMORIAL

Step lightly, God, you used to live here.
Before our people began turning everything
into little pieces of gold and diamond.
Into the green note that is only sandpaper.
Return, and find your place among the living,
among the stubborn living.
Death still lingers here with us.

My eyes water each time I recall your presence.
Other peoples' gods died in the war;
their guarding angels were massacred
the day the bombs began to reign.
You know that the Harmattan winds
blow dust upon what memories I bring.

The sacrifices I offer were gathered
from the ashes in the blazing flames
of our town just before the killing fields
were laid waste at the hand of the one
who still carries the axe with a bloody eye.

You drew me out of the muddy streams
along Duport Road, where
the stench of death still hangs on to life.
When you see the road curving
at Alfred Musa Hill, the scent will knock
you out, God, the scent will knock you out.
Tread softly, many still lie there.

You know, I shudder each time I recall
the carcasses of my brothers and my sisters,
each time I return to the memories
of those who refused to rot.

Did I see that, God, did you see me see that?

The smell of death held on to my soiled skirt
lest I forgot the thousands and the feasting dogs.
Dogs have had their say,

for once, dogs have had their say, God.
When you see the town below, walk softly
so the bones do not talk back to you.
Bones own the town now, God.

REBURIAL: TO LAMENT OF DRUMS

This is the Reburial season; the Reburial rites
must accompany the dead. So the spirit of the great
can ascend and take his place on the Ancestral Stool.
But all the rice in the attic has become straw.
Layers and layers of rice bundles from the fields
have become only shells of chaff.

They say the night following our father's death,
light footsteps of rats and farm mice
and squirrels and groundhogs and roaches
and bats and crawling creatures from space,
and flying creatures unknown
and whatever it was, could be heard
in the dawn hours of the night.

That time when only animals may wander under
the dark moon. The Reburial must feast
on rice and wine and cane juice and palm wine
and rivers of imported gin and all kinds
of soft drinks. The Reburial needs antelopes
and deer and half smoked bush-hog legs
and *tabadu* and large quantities

of dried fish from the ocean, kuta fish, shark,
salmon, fresh cavalla, and crab meats,
shrimp of all kinds. We must have fresh oil
from virgin palm trees, fresh red oil with the smell
of dawn upon its breath.
When *Kwee* comes to town, he will demand of us
all the fruit in and out of season.
There should be oranges in plenty,

bananas and plantains, ripe as virgins, pineapples
and butter pears, breadnuts and breadfruit.
We will need drums of white, red and pink kola nuts.
There must be all sorts of nuts to display.
When *Kwee* comes singing at the village outskirts,
all the young men must line up
with strong muscular chests, high shoulders as men,
ready for war. All the virgins will then
scatter themselves under their mothers' roofs,

the women, sitting still in dark huts and the drums,
pounding so hard. All over the world, people will
hear, and know that it is not only *Kwee* in town.
It is not only the *Town Crier's* wailing
the ground fears so; it is not just the silence
of the virgins and their mothers
behind closed doors that the night fears so.
And it is not the men, ready for war
that make the ground tremble.

The Reburial is here, under the *Tuwah-Kai,*
so the plank has been laid. The elders must
assemble with long *Kaflahs,* the *Bodior,* ahead.
There must be plenty of white rice, pestled
by young girls, ready to be initiated into
the marriage of the world. We will need horn
blowers to sound the *Poo-lee-peh-leh-wlee.*
Bring in drummers from your best.

Let go of the *Klan-klan-teh* so the shores
of Harper roll into the shores of Greenville, into
the shores of Buchanan, into the shores of Monrovia,
into the shores of Robertsport.
The Atlantic's surging and rolling will be a sight.
Foaming waters, uneasy, and the creatures of the deep,
dancing for the reburial that is here.

And then we'll sit with kola-nut bowls, we the initiate,
the fathers of elders, we the mothers of ancestors.
But after three years, The Reburial has not come.
The Plank cannot be laid without the feast,
without the calling of the towns, without the rice
bundles, emptied in waiting. There are your virgins

now, scattered abroad, and the young men
who went to war have become like fine beasts.
They say, we do not dance with the feet of spirits;
it is the spirits that watch the dance.
We do not dance with the feet of the dead
or the feet of men with blood on their palms.
We do not need the hands of human carvers.
We do not need the hands of murderers.

IV

Poems from:
THE RIVER IS RISING
AUTUMN HOUSE PRESS, 2007

I will bring back my exiled people...
they will rebuild the ruined cities and live in them...
—AMOS 9:14

The River Is Rising

a song for Liberian women

The river is rising, and this is not a flood.
After years of drought, the ground, hardened

and caked in blood, in dry places, here we are, today.

Riverbanks are swelling with the incoming tide,
coming in from the Atlantic just beyond the ridge

of rolling hills and rocks in Monrovia.

Finally, here we stand at the banks!
Finally, here we are, see how swiftly

the tide rushes in to fill the land with salt.

Fish and crabs and the huge clams and shrimps—
all the river's creatures are coming in with the tide.

The river is rising, but this is not a flood.

Do not let your eye wander away from this scene.
Yes, all the bones below the Mesurado or the St. Paul

or Sinoe or the Loffa River will be brought up
to land so all the overwhelming questions
can once more overwhelm us.

But they are bringing in our lost sister
on a high stool, and there she stands, waving at those

who in refusing to die, simply refused to die.

This is not a song for Ellen alone. This is a song
for Mapue and Tenneh and all the Ellens there are.

This is a song for Kimah and Musu and Massa.

This is for Nyeneplue and Nyenoweh, for Kou and Glayee
and Korto, for the once solitary woman of war.

This is a song so Wani will also dance.

This is a song for that small girl-child who came out
just this morning. They are still seeking a name

to call her—a river name, a name from the water
and from the fire too. That solitary mother in flight

will no longer birth her child by the roadside
where shells were her baby's first bed.

Let the womb quiver!
Let church bells jingle!
Let hundreds of drums pound, *Klan-klan-teh*!
Let men bring out old trumpets
so the wind will take flight!

Let that small pepper bird on the tree branch
cry and sing no more the solitary song.

Let the Mesurado behind my home or what was
my home or still is or maybe, maybe, who cares?

The river is rising, but this is not a flood.

Let no man stand between us
and the river again!

In the Ruined City: A Poem for Monrovia

In the Ruined City, the water flaps lightly
against the beach at night.
It is August, after too many years,
the rain still pours down like stones.
The Atlantic always knows when to go to sleep,
but all the girls roam dark nights
and men have forgotten they are still men.

Monrovia has lost its name.

The ocean roars like wild fire.
It roars like a hungry lion at dawn,
like the whirlwind.
In the ruined city, all the girls
have legs made from plastic weapons,
and the boys pretend it is okay
for the once beautiful girls to walk
around on plastic legs.
There is little time for weeping,

and all the world stands silent.

There are no more trumpets or drums.
The dancer who lost his legs
in the war now sits by the roadside, waiting.
It is something to lose your legs to a war,
they say, to Charles Taylor's ugly war,
where the fighter cannot recall why he still fights.

The men have forgotten they used to be men,
and the women sit by the roadside wondering
what has happened to this land.
If those outside of here do not come,
Liberia will drown in this rain.
Outside my window, the rain taps hard
in Old Road Sinkor, for my homecoming.

Only the rain knows how to cry.

CITY

At night, it is like fire
spreading beneath us.
This vast city
aflame, and the plane
groaning.

The city is more beautiful
from the sky at night.
At noon, it looks like
a worn-out garage,
a thing in the middle
of swamp country.

All the buildings are worn-out,
rusted to the bone
of steel, twisted
to make way so life
can go on.

Everything is bent and broken
along the hilltops.
I touch air to see if air
is still there.
The touchdown,

and we appear all worn-out,
too, like the city, broken.
All the birds
moved out long ago.
The trees too.

An Elegy for the St. Peter's Church Massacred

I fled the war in that first ceasefire.
Missing all the other wars, the other massacres,
the burning and re-burning of Monrovia,

the silencing again of those who had already
been silenced in that first sweep.
My neighbors envied me through dark-eyed lashes,
skeletal cheekbones, and hunger.

I envy those who were massacred.
Those who never saw their killers approach
with heavy boot steps that made no sound
in the dark morning hours.

Those who died in colonies, in one huge group
at the *President's* order.
They arrived in death, holding hands—
mothers, hugging their babies, men,
helping their wives over the hills of death;
talking, laughing, singing,
they walked happily in death.

It is such a good thing to go with company.

The Atlantic's wailing winds at the hurried steps
of hundreds of soldier boots
will live forever with the living.

I honor those who were massacred
at St. Peter's Lutheran by troops
with only an errand to run.
The raining of guns upon sleeping people
as if this were not already July.

How I envy those who never heard those
stalking boot steps at the church doors that night;
never saw the faces of their murderers,
never had to count the hours remaining—
only one shot, and it was all over.

When we wept with Glayee, who arrived
clinging to two toddler girls at Soul Clinic
Refugee camp, how could I envy her?
Haunted eyes, scarred arms and legs from
climbing up that barbed wire fence, a slash wrist
for where they spilled her own blood
in sacrificial offering.

It is a sad story when we survive the massacre
of hundreds who were only sleeping before God.
It is a sad story when one survives
the massacre of the whole world like that.

THE MORNING AFTER: AN ELEGY

My husband and I gather our remaining lives
the morning after. I snatch away memories
of childhood, adolescence, college, where my life

was a bittersweet of books, boys, my father's
discipline, politics, and the whole world spread
out, awaiting me. This morning's bombing

is again rocking our lives and our home. A single
suitcase will have to bear all this pain.
It is August 1,1990, right after a number no

one could count were massacred in deep sleep;
today, taken before today. They lay all over
St. Peter's Lutheran, in the aisles, on the solid

wood pulpit, twisted, in classrooms on top of one
another, a child here, a mother there, a father here,
a baby there, a heap here, a few there, our tattered

history. Where was God at two o'clock in the morning?
How did those soldiers push aside church doors,
reason, God? And is there anyone who can tell

my wide-eyed children how a single order could
put hundreds to death? To explain how hundreds
of troops could empty hundreds of bullets while

the world sits by? So, we pack boxes of books, pots,
suitcases of clothes, stereos; we fold mattresses
and chairs, shutting blinds, windows, turning

off waterless taps so if water ever returns while
we're gone, this home will not become a river.
These new circumstances of our lives now gather

mucus in my throat. All this time, our three starving dogs are watching; no barking, no jumping, are they also wondering if someone will explain where

we're going? One last wave for my watchdogs before refugee camps, starvation, then flight for America. But everyone couldn't come to America, you see.

SOMETHING DEATH CANNOT KNOW

My husband and I stole away from the camp one day
to see if it was now safe to come back home, from the war.

We pushed open double oak doors, and in our living
room, a few pots laid here and there; no water,
no lights, no clothing—everything gone.

Outside, you could count the deep rocket holes.
Splinters from fallen rockets could fill buckets
after months of bombing.

I stood in the middle of what used to be my hallway, my
house, my world, counting holes on the walls;
the house now leaked. Windows, partly blown out.

On the floor, my Sunday dresses lay trashed about, where
looters had dropped them in that sudden rush.
I watched the sun come in, through cracked glass

of windows, through the holes in the walls, where
only missile splinters could have passed—
But I was home again.

When I saw the birds, they chirped and began to fly
from overgrown brushes. Then the wind blew
in from the river, cold November winds from the river.

The Atlantic's moist winds from the other side over
the hills from the beach, where the ocean's restless waves
howl away days.

The scent of sweet blossoms, oregano mix,
and mint in the air. Flowers in what used to be my yard,
wild. I sat on the floor,

on the cold ceramic tiles of what used to be my living room
and laughed loud, hard, until my husband rushed inside
to see if I was still okay.

I laughed until I began to weep. Glad to be alive, to be here,
to know a town that had become ghost, to get acquainted
with the birds and the flowers and the river

and the winds for the first time. To know life
in its subtle creeping—when only crickets matter.

To know that after all this, my children were still alive,
that Mama was alive still, and life remembered
I used to live here.

The sun touching my now flabby arms told me I was here.
After all that bombing, here was I.
To know that there is something death cannot know—

Coming Home

for Besie-Nyesuah

Besie runs towards me, arms wide, despite the crowd
at the airport, she's screaming, "Mo-mm-m-m-ie,"

and everybody stares. Arms around me, my daughter
holds me tight, and we almost fall beside her suitcase

I have just lifted off the belt. At nineteen, she is now
a woman, tall, slender, her soft, small arms and fair skin

remind me of Ma Wadeh, my mother-in-law. In a moment,
I am looking her all over, counting to see if she is not

too skinny for a girl her age. Every girl becomes woman
when she can come home, knowing how like her mother

she is becoming—a woman like all the other women
before her. "This is Pittsburgh," I say, "isn't it beautiful?"

We're driving past houses in the distant hills along
Pittsburgh's winding freeway, houses that lean and rush

past us as we also rush past them. Everything here leans
sideways, almost free, as if to fall into the merging rivers

down below. My college-age children are coming home
to Pennsylvania, where we are surrounded by hills

and valleys and cliffs, and the university where my
new students speak with an accent they refuse to admit.

"So this is home now?" Besie says as if to herself
while I turn into our new driveway in a neighborhood

of rolling hills and brick houses overlooking one another.
"We are the first black on this property," I say. But this

is going to be home—all these valleys and green, green hills
will be home. "But this is Pennsylvania," Besie says, as doors

bang and everyone rushes out to welcome her home after
too many months away. "We are all trying to find home,"

I say, as my words become lost in the din of screaming
children and my husband, lifting Besie up in the air

and swinging her around in circles. All my children
are under one roof again, I tell myself, for the first

time, all my children are under one roof in our new state.
But Michigan is that ghost that stands at the outskirts

of your new town, where your memory refuses to shut out
so many years, and that year when you arrived with

nothing and looking to find home among strangers,
where the cold, cold winds became a new friend.

Your second chance at finding home, now becoming
memory too. Michigan haunts the holidays, another

ghost to carry around among all the other ghosts we are
seeking to undo. In Monrovia, families will gather

and discuss the many years we have been away from
home. Monrovia is the true ghost story of lost peoples

in the Diaspora. In America, we are the new nomads,
the wanderers coming home or looking to make

home or running away from home among new people,
and one by one, our children, who will never know

where we really come from, are leaving only to come
back to decorative lights, Christmas trees, holiday

music, and turkey baking in the oven, stuffing,
and pies. We are becoming new people, I tell myself.

When My Daughter Tells Me
She Has a Boyfriend

When my daughter tells me she has a boyfriend now,
at college, where we send our children so they can
grow up some more, I ask her, "Is he black… or…
white…?" There is just silence, no phone clicking,
no whisper. No pauses are allowed between a mother
and her daughter who has gone to college
to find herself among many lost people.

"What sort of question is that," she sighs.
The phone has learned how to talk back
in many ways. "Is he tall or short? Are his eyes
large and round and brown like the walnut
just before it becomes meal? Are they green-green
or are they blue, pale, after the color of sky
just before gray settles in upon them in September?"
"Mom…" my daughter is weeping now.
My daughter has learned to weep at last
about the things that really matter.

"Are you racist?" My daughter cries into the phone.
Only a phone knows how to ask such questions.
It is only a faraway phone, a faraway daughter
taking liberty with phones, asking
a perfect mother if she is racist.

"Racism is something that happens to me," I say.
Doesn't a mother have the right to know,
to know it all, to have it all plain and simple on the table,
all the things one needs to know?
Whether my daughter is bringing home a tall
black boy, so dark, his skin sparkles,
a boy with hair he spends many nights
grooming so it loses all its nappy?

But my daughter tells me she's going home
with her boyfriend—home to his mother,
another woman, a white woman who will
stand at her doorstep hugging

my first girl child, the daughter of a bull,
Jabbeh *Cho, Koo-oo-koo-oo,* an off-shoot
of *Nganlun,* where the spring water bubbles
at noonday in March. My daughter from
Seo Paton, the woman from Wah, losing her way
in a land where we are all trying to find ourselves.

My daughter, the women from *Seo* are hot like pepper.
They do not run off to meet their boyfriend's mother
just like that, girl. But in America,
a girl can hop on a car or plane, on a truck, or whatever
to meet her boyfriend's family at eighteen,
before her mother has looked the boy over,

before the elders sit in upon the whole idea
of a boyfriend, to see if it's taboo to marry a boy
from another clan. "What are his people like?
Who is his father? Does his father come from
a great people, a great clan?" I wanted to ask.

In America, a child at eighteen can drive a car,
run over a deer at two o'clock in the morning,
gather their belongings at noon, and move
out, at sixteen. I have heard it all.

My girl-child whose beauty shines like the moon,
over the hilltops, over the forest when
the sun comes out in December, in Tugbakeh.
Nyeneplu, the beautiful, my daughter
running off to meet the other woman,
my daughter who reminds me of Neferteri
on her throne. My daughter, a woman like myself.
When I see that boy, I will cook him spicy pepper soup
so he knows how the dodo cries at night
just before the hawk has time to flee.

Leaving: A Poem for Gee

Today, Gee shows me what it means to pick up and leave.
Boxes on top of boxes, where a shoelace refuses to stay

in a teenager's moving-away storage. "Mom," he says,
"the next time we move away to a new town, find

a new church for singing and clapping and youth groups,
where everyone cares where you're going when you

have to leave. Talk to someone please, Mom, talk to
someone who knows someone in the new church, in

that new town, and in that neighborhood so there is
someone to speak to when I arrive, and when I have

to leave, so there will be someone I can leave behind."
Sometimes, night can be like that you see, the invisible

act, the disappearing people we are, when like dark
shadows or the moon and the fireflies, suddenly, we are

no longer there, and yet no one wonders. In another few
days, we will be gone from this small town of unfamiliar

people who never knew we were even passing through
like this. In Byron Center, where we used to live—that

small Michigan Dutch town of small houses, a church
here, a church there, kind people with old stories of having

arrived on ships in the World War. A town where no one
ever went anywhere because now, they all belonged.

My next-door neighbor's father used to own his house
before him, after his great-grandfather died, leaving

him the house. Small town, small secrets, huge memories,
where the ground is hardened not by anger alone. I am

that other stranger seeking to find roots and ground
and a place where even the squirrel can run free, where

the squirrel also belongs to me. War is such a mystery,
such an unexplained phenomenon, an unexplained

grassland, the indefensible stories of seekers. But no one
clings to those seeking for that new homeland, where

memory can find place again. Outside my house, people
refuse to take on to the newcomer or see or ask questions.

They made their friends long ago while I was still in
the Liberian war or before I was even born. So when

I move away tomorrow, I will leave behind only a house
on a bare street corner, where flowers bloom not just

in the spring, a place where the cherry tree at my
front yard blooms pink petals every spring and sheds

them thoughtlessly in the rain, and the green lawn across
the road sits quietly, and the neighbors, mute as death.

The Golden Retriever barks all night long, as the cricket
loses track of its own singing. Big mounds of iron hills

rolling, and the neighbor woman's child presses her nose
against the window glass, my invisible neighbor.

I am leaving behind no one at all, don't get me wrong;
this is the new life where only the ghost lives. I am the

blessed one with just one small daughter and a son, a
husband, another son, and another daughter, taken

by the wind. Someone once asked me why people like us
move around so much; why can't we balance feet between

the hills and the sloping crevasses of this new life, between
these old cliffs and the valleys, and I say, "I do not know."

BRINGING CLOSURE

Closure is such a final thing—the needle in the arm,
one last word or no last word at all, a death chamber

where the supposed convict lies waiting so the poison
will descend or ascend to the heart, a final beat,

and then sleep, that eternal thing none of us living
has ever seen. In California, today, a man is being

put to death, but outside, his supporters wait; candles,
flames, anger—the cold chill of death and life,

and a country that waits for all the arguments to die
or live on. The victim's mother will see closure today,

they say, and move on after the murderer or the supposed
murderer is laid to rest with her son, side by side.

Death is such an ironic thing to know. To know death
is to know rot, hush, the lack of pain. It is three a.m.

in Pennsylvania. Time, so deceptive, and arbitrary
and imperfect. Around the world, we all wait, for

the executioner's poke into vein, blood meeting poison.
We are such civilized people, I'd say, dishing out death

in small poking needles. The newsmen tell us they
cannot find his vein. The awkwardness of asking the one

awaiting death to find his own vein so they can murder
him too—the executioner's awkward fingers, the knowing

fingers—afraid of both the man and the art of killing the man.
I hate death. I hate the dying, the ugly process of dying,

the ritual of murder. So I too, keep vigil on my carpet.
Tomorrow, I'll tell my eleven-year-old daughter how

we have all murdered another human being. An eye
for an eye, so far away from my bedroom of dim lights,

a comforter or two, the surrounding hills in close view.
There is always a mountain here in Pennsylvania,

always that looming presence of life and death and the
faraway feeling of the valley below, of being so far away

from home. There is no closure, I see, after the poison
has reached the heart, and the accused, stretched out, finally.

The victim's mother begins to weep all over again—
as if this was just the beginning of the dying.

At Point Loma

At Point Loma, a student may dip a toe or two in
the ocean, in between classrooms and teachers, in

between falling in and out of love, between the pages
of a book's silence. On a fast day, the windy air, misty,

salty, so much beauty for the eyes, and I'd say, what a life!
In my small, Pennsylvania town, old railroad tracks

still wind their way around Altoona, old steel country,
rusting away from lack of use, the green mountains,

rising like clumps of dirt mounds. Altoona, where
some will never understand how a student can learn

anything sitting on a beach. But in San Diego, the
hotel suite, where my kind hosts have lavished this

undeserving luxury upon me, a suite that hangs over
the bay, the lovely balcony frightens me though.

What if I slip and fall into this old bay where a man
rises out of his boat at dawn as if he were a fish?

His wheelbarrow, squeaking with things he is hauling
on to his boat on the bay. There are so many boats,

the water has no air to breathe; the air has no water
to drink. There is so much in this life to live for,

and yet my boat neighbors have chosen to live on
the water, not on the shoreline, on the sand, or on

the bare cliffs where Point Loma University, so
blessed, sits along the peaceful shoreline as if waiting

for God. This is the sort of place that follows
the traveler around forever, like the old stories *Iyeeh*

told me in Dolokeh. I am not one to fall in love
with a place so easily, but somehow, I cannot help

smiling at these palms, this foliage, these people,
or this wind that takes me way back home where

these shrubberies also grow wild in Monrovia.
I wonder what was on God's mind, San Diego, when

he made you? This sort of place makes my soul cry
for that other shoreline so far away, where home sits

by the sea, waiting, too, where the ocean is wild and hot.

MONROVIA REVISITED

This is the city that killed my mother.
Its crooked legs bent
from standing too long,
waiting so angry people can kill
themselves too.

No more grass along street corners—
so many potholes from years of war.
Immigrants from all over the globe
used to come here
on tender feet,

in search of themselves.
Abandoned city—
a place that learned
how to cry out loud even though
nobody heard.

This is the city where I first learned
how to lose myself.
Windy city, blue ocean city.
They say a city on the hill
cannot be hid.

The city of salty winds, salty tears,
where stubborn people still hold
us hostage after Charles Taylor.
You should come here if you want
to know how sacred
pain can be.

AUGUST 11, 2003

I sit at the edge of my bed where the bedroom
is another place in which one may go into oneself.

Charles Taylor and his family are boarding
a plane in Monrovia.
On TV, Charles Taylor is climbing
on to a jetliner,
leaving.

Someone has decided he should leave on a plane,
not by drowning or by a bullet, not by
an explosion or by execution.

Someone has given him a beautiful place
where he can sit and smoke
and toast a drink to the hundreds of thousands
he has already killed.

The phone beside my bed is ringing.

All over the world, phones are ringing
themselves mute in solemn duty—
All over the world,
phones are ringing today.

But the words of my heart have become
lost thoughts. Fourteen years,
and I'm like a dead woman.

My heart has a big hole where all the
stories no one has heard, linger forever.
Where stories become scarred,

where there is no solace
for the grieved and the dead.

When my father finally comes through,
the phone seems dead—only the muffles
of his weary voice.

After fourteen years, my father has also
lost his voice to describe the years.

In a Moment When the World Stops

One solemn moment a star falls
through sky like fireflies.
What was it you said when the bomb exploded
in Oklahoma, and in a moment, hundreds who did not
call in sick for work that day lay among rubble,
in between stubborn walls and steel,
walls becoming plain dirt?

The day my husband told me to give the rest
of my life in all of its bareness of plain laughter,
to go to bed on the same bed beside him and bear
our children and be his friend forever, I smiled,
not knowing. In the restaurant, I stared at the walls
to see if anything would move.
Did anything dare to move that day?

When the plane is in mid-sky and over the Atlantic,
or when pilot and crew have no clue where it is,
passengers resting at dawn,
a watch somewhere ticks and moves with the plane,
and then suddenly, a voice announces how
in a moment this plane will be gone,
the voice summing up every
living breath on the plane the way

a mathematician adds figures on a bare sheet.
That everyone should prepare for the crash,
prepare to go down somewhere into uncharted
territory. That moment of eye meeting soul,
between passengers and crew,
the clock's minute hand takes the moment
away, and the moment refuses to be explained.

How a baby's miniature hand may rest upon
a mother's, white sheets, white walls, white
everything, the infant's eyes, so unsure
of the world, and the world standing still too?
Today, like a child, I stand beside my husband
as always, in the hospital room as he lies still,

in preparation for the landing.
A parachute can bear the weight of a man
at the onset of midlife.

They will cut his skin aside, dark skin, then red, fat
and all, peeled away by white hands.
The doctor will again prove how we are all alike inside.
Eye, meeting eye, my husband grins,
words slipping into thin air, where words
can let a woman down. I will be here
when you wake up, I say,
I will be here when you wake up, I say.

After the Memorial

Today, another student died at school. Another boy
at twenty, another sophomore, another woman's only son.

A girl in my class told me the news just before my ten
o'clock class. She said, it was his heart—a bad heart.

Something that was always a part of him, she said.
Something in his heart was always loose—a thin line

somewhere. Where the heart was supposed to tighten
to pump blood from the heart to the brain to the hands

to the feet and belly buttons to the toes and back again
to the heart. Something must have snapped, she said.

Stephanie, a girl almost looking nineteen or twenty
or twenty-one or something. Bloody eyes, red hair, she

stood at my desk in tears, there she stood. Was I the priest
or counselor or something? The delicate lines already

making their way under her eyelids. This was her friend,
her boyfriend, her best friend. He was tall and blond

and smart and funny and walked like he'd bought the campus
and the whole world with just his looks. Someone told me

afterwards, it was heroin overdose and alcohol overdose
and everything overdose. No one called the police.

In a college dorm, where the party can run over the rim
of every glass and the fumes from everything everywhere

in the party room can penetrate every fabric of everything
alive, and everyone is red-eyed because something

else is smelling. And you know it is often too late to call
the police or the ambulance, and of course, not his parents.

He was supposed to come to, they'd said, on the floor where
everybody left him so he could come to. Last year, another

student died—my student—at home, in a bed that belonged
to him, where the sheets and the mattress were soft

and white and cool and personal. The sheets understood
the matter more plainly. They belonged to him. It was drug

overdose, someone said. When the news came on the phone,
I was at home. Tuesday—not a day for news. The Dean from

campus called to break the news to me. Why me, I thought.
I was scared. His mom had asked to break the news gently

to this one teacher. She will take it hard, and my son loved
her like family, she'd said. I rushed to my bathroom, my

stomach boiling when I heard. All the hours I'd spent
tutoring this one kid until his writing skills which had nothing

to do with his writing skills, sharpened. His words had taken
on color and detail and precision just so he would die?

He had died quietly in his sleep, I was told. At the college
dinner after the memorial, his mom held my hand tight,

staring. "He was our only child, you know." Silence.
"I understand completely," I said. "I understand incompletely."

While I Wait for the War

I used to say, "When the war ends, we will go back home."
To the sea and the river, where the humid sun turns miles
of marshland behind my house into solid ground.
At night, the moon lends light to my chicken coop.

Back home, where it's okay when your Auntie you've
never ever seen comes in, speaking impeccable Grebo,
talking of how she carried you on her back when you
were just this tall, cleaned your pupu bottom,

ate the snot from your nose when you had the cold, then
whipped your butt because you couldn't stop using
those four-letter words. Now she comes wanting money
to zinc her roof, a house she was building before
your Ma first met your Pa.

Home, where the home is a mansion, but the road that leads
there winds up and down forgotten, rocky hills no car can climb.
Where the president's mistress is your college classmate,
but it's okay, because he's president, you know.

At home if you're not careful, you can find your own head
right on your door step in the morning, before the rooster
crows, your head left there by the president's men,
but it's still okay. Where *Bai* was your grandfather,

boasting of all the warriors who fought to give him this land
he thought he owned until he was dead and gone.
Now come some rebels with guns....
So, I sit on the carpet here in America, the way
a Grebo woman sits on *The Mat*,

my legs stretched out, and I holler, crying because today
the phone told me that Ma had died at home, two weeks ago,
and I didn't even know. I get up after one long hour of crying,
go to the window and cry some more.

On the streets in Byron Center, cars still speed, people
still mow their lawns, water their fresh, green grass
just to mow again tomorrow. My neighbors wash,
then wax their cars; wash, then wax their cars.
Today, you know, Ma Nmano's news came in, dead,

my mother dead, and I'm here waiting for the war
at the window, my blouse wet. I cry loud, then low, when
news comes in that Nyanken Hne is dead, and Sunny, too,
dead, everyone, dead. I cry one dirge after the other,
for Uncle Henry Toe who died just after the cease-fire,

couldn't wait to see Taylor crowned president. Cry for T.K.,
executed for being a policeman, for Ma Nandi,
my mother-in-law in the Ivory Coast, who refused to die
on foreign ground. For *Borbor* Kweesay, Sehseh Kimah...

and after eight years, I'm still crying dirges.
So I a buy a house, a car, to look like I'm settling, to replace
what the war took away. I write a book for everyone
to read the stories.... Sometimes I want to just get up
and walk back home.

Where the dodo still wakes us in Tugbakeh and the hawk
enters the chicken coop on a farm far away at *Gbaliahde*,
and we children run because the roosters are ready for battle
with the hawk for snatching away one of theirs.
In the market, you can buy fish between clattering voices,

returning home with the morning news, fresh
from the lips of market women. I've come back to school
to read more books... to write about my children turning
into foreigners right under my roof.
They eat beef, roasted in spicy-hot pepper.

I stew them cassava leaves, palaver sauce cooked in red palm
oil from Ghana, gari from Nigeria. My house smells of Africa,
Asia, and America while my children grow like coconut trees.
They eat palm butter on steamed rice, okra stewed with
smoked fish, pig's feet and shrimp—

then eat ice cream on Dutch apple pie. My children swallow
fufu in spicy pepper soup, then stand there,
rocking to American Hip-Hop, while I wait for the war.
In the meantime, they will grow up without the *Dorklor*,

without the pounding of dozens of drums, where the dancer
always knows which beat to dance to. While *Gborbelloh*
throws us under great illusions, dancers blow dust about.
Without *Iyeeh's* spider tales, weaving a hundred webs
from which any of us may dangle free.

FOR MA NMANO JABBEH: A DIRGE

Hne Nmano, *Sagba-Nyene*, I come to you singing
long after you were gone. Your brown beauty
and sad laughter remain here forever.
I still see you standing there in the middle
of the house; your Grebo-English voice, like fire
in the March sunshine of tropical farm burning.
So when the rains come, rice farmers
will plant single rice grains in tiny holes
over acres of charcoal-ash ground.

In late February, the farmer dreads the coming
of early rains. They say we do not eat with the same
heaviness of heart we took to brush the farmland
with which we felled the oak. How did you let
the war overwhelm you so? How could you let
the world speed you so early away in its swift winds?
The world, where you were the one that made
daylight come so quickly. My father was the king
only you could fashion with your soft,
swift palms under pungent spices.

Mother of mothers, the mother I could never have—
the one who could take a lone child in, and yet, leave
her sitting at the doorpost. I'm still singing dirges
for you, *Sagba*. I call on you to wake up because
day has broken through the fields.
The sun's rays have come penetrating the years,
and yet you sleep. I long again to see your
solemn complexity, your anger and your
fear of drawing too close to the stepdaughter.

I spread out *lappas* for you under the December
sky while the grass is still wet—*lappas* upon *lappas*
carpet my driveway while dawn comes in with fresh
dew upon my lawn, and at night, bats cannot hide
under the eaves of my roof of tarred shingles
in stranger land. How does a daughter lay out
The Mat just to wail alone? When our brothers put
The Mat down, mourners come

from faraway towns, wailing for the Warrior
Woman's passing. It is the son that must put down
The Mat so the *Nehwordeh* will sit and wail.
So our brothers' wives, our *Bai-de* can show off
their sweet dirges in winding tones.
So our men can prove to us, *Nehwordeh*, their
manhood, and then under the burial tent, you can
hear the elders in their *Bati-oh-Bati*, proverbs,
rising out of ancestral lands.

Then from hut to hut, we spread out your *lappas*
from the years on the verandas. So the coming
mourners can come and see what a life
you once had. It is the kola nut then that welcomes
the stranger among us kin.
But now, all your sons and our brothers
are gone before you. Where will passersby learn
our town's history? Where will the women,
singing dirges to you find a place
to stretch out and wail?

Hne Nmano, Townswoman, for whom men
will go to war. How is it you left before the town
could gather? Before the *Town Crier* was conceived
after the killing of the *Town Crier*?
I am the child who missed her way into
your possession, and sat in, even though you
did not want me. Did the war teach you at last
that the owl does not have to wail at the setting
of the sun before the sun sets?

The rooster crows only for its own coming day,
but we think it is for us that the rooster
flaps strong wings upon a tree stump to crow?
At the Springs Payne Airfield while the plane
waited, there you were, clinging to me, singing
a dirge for your own burial.
Sagba, the one that could take my leopard father
by the horns, and let him follow
wherever you went.

IN THE MAKING OF A WOMAN

In the making of a woman,
the naval string is cut, ears pierced,
and the beads firmly tied
around her waist, neck, ankles.
Iyeeh does not give in to the infant's loud screaming.
After all, she must be made a woman
in every sense that a Grebo woman can be.

Then the naming ritual must begin.
The recounting of histories
she may never hear repeated
except the day she brings forth
another like herself.
Nothing must go wrong here,
not even a sneeze.
The ceremony, with perfection
if she must be a woman.

And then, though with beads strung
all over her, *Iyeeh* calls
in the elders, and the libation begins.
Chanting so solemnly, the baby in her
quits screaming, and she is let
upon the world—a Grebo woman
is let loose upon our innocent world.

TABOO

Arrangements for my coming
into the world
are incomplete pieces

of letters and promises,
a clause that ends with a cough,
a deep sigh

in the middle of a sentence,
that one sentence
that was not said—

the knowing and not knowing
how other girls left
their babies

in buckets and outdoor toilets,
went to school the next day
with well-ironed

skirts, combed hair, and a smile.
I was the word you didn't say—

strong-willed fetus,
refusing

to go away, the half dried
lappa on the clothesline
in April.

And Mama,
the dropout,
just so I could be
me.

A WINDING TRAIL

My mother carried me upside down, pushed me out
            like a crab, sideways.

The children in our town could not place my name in line
            with other names. All those *Iyeeh*

who could not sing my praise names right, mumbled
            each time I passed. My naming ritual stood still

so thunder would roll. Libation waiting, the kola nuts
slowly bleeding the bowl of water, red. Out of nowhere,

a mucus-face child sneezed, and *Iyeeh* mumbled about
the kinds of spices, the mix of peppers she'd grounded

            into the ceremonial blend of pungent,
eye-watering pepper; how long she'd rubbed the lump

            upon the pepper rock; hot pepper seeds
crushed by *Iyeeh's* old hands.

            God, you know how an old woman
will carry on about a thing like that?

The clansman from my father's town arrived; feet dusty,
            sweat, streaming down his dark face even though

it was just dawn. The calabash of libation fell and broke,
            and *Bai* forgot what my name was to be.

"*Lahwloh,*" *Bai* shook his head.
            Lahwloh—to calm my mother's heart,

"be patient in this life," the elders bowed their heads—
                        Absolute consent.
The Oracles agreed, and I becoming, *Lahwloh-Jlajeh*

Libation—chanting,
libation—chanting.

So may it be, in unison, the elders and the oracles,

and then I screamed when someone slapped my bottom.
                    This was a lack of reverence
coming from a newborn, someone said. *Iyeeh* bowed

and chuckled at a stone on the rocky ground—
I would make a tough wife someday, *Iyeeh* said.

All these years, *Iyeeh* tells this story still, in winding trails.
One day, it was the washing water that was spilled,

a boy's, not a girl's sneeze. It was lightning that caused
                    the spill, not the clansman or the sneeze.
My life has been a winding trail.

You want to know my past, don't you, God?

I grew up, spreading legs and arms in all directions,
like the pawpaw tree behind *Iyeeh's* hut.

"A coconut tree never grows flesh if it must grow so tall,"
        Iyeeh says. And then I met my father—light-light

skinned like the inside of a pumpkin. His hair looking
                    as if it had been washed in palm oil,
dabbled over the fire for a shine, flattened to his scalp.

Where was he while I grew?
                    Lahwloh, a lone stump,
all my roots clipped so other trees would grow.

STORIES

Someone will tell my story when I'm gone.
Someone will come into my house and look
at all these boxes on top of each other,
and all these papers I have wanted
to write something on.
The stories I carry around like a pregnant woman
who cannot say when she got pregnant—
They will be spilled all over
in invisible tidbits. People will say how
she was this and how she was that,

but no one will know all the stories I carry around
like a garbage truck.
The stories that coil like an earthworm
after the rain. The sight of an earthworm—
something not only children will scream at.
Maybe someone will write them for me—
The stories about my brother, Toh,
crashing my father's yellow taxi
with my father seated right there beside him.

The taxi wanting to protect Toh from
my father's anger—the taxi that was meant
to set Toh on that career track at last.
Pa, always wanting to turn little people's
dreams into his own. Carving our lives
as though we were some pieces of wood
or wood dust on his carving table.
And the other stories, the ones about
me beating up that boy just because
he called me *Marie Biscuit.*

All the other neighborhood children
standing there while we still lived on the Bye Pass.
Me, beating up a boy, and Pa,
laughing and clapping when he heard
how his daughter had gone and beat up a strong boy.
One woman that will beat up the boys,
Pa said, laughing and walking to his room,
looking like a small child coming home
with his first prize trophy. But yet, there
are the other stories nobody will ever know.

STRANGER WOMAN

In the village, the old women pull her out,
the afterbirth and all. She is dashed into

wrinkled, welcoming hands, then a warm *lappa*
embraces her as the old women chant praise names

from here to faraway places, and then the blessings.
Iyeeh ties up, then snaps off the naval string, then

washes the newborn woman who is screaming
throat, tongue, and guts out. Then the beading

begins—wrists, ankles, neck, waist, all stringed
up. This new woman, who is now bound.

After that, the piercing of soft ears so earrings will
pass through. Little black threads strung in place

until the earrings arrive. Then the naming is done,
and maybe there'll be a Rooster's Feather

stuck in her dark, curly hair, and she's betrothed
to some man, who himself is only a child.

He may never discover how she was destined
to recreate or destroy him someday. In the village,

you may find her walking to school, after discarding
those birthing beads for puberty, her breasts

sharp like needles, or maybe, on the farm road,
she walks, now married before the breasts

are even formed, practicing on the way to market,
dirges she will sing at the funeral of her father-in-law

whom she dislikes terribly. In the city, you may
find the stranger woman who is so many girls

at the same time; in college, or a high school
dropout; maybe, a single mother who takes home

the latest baby to her mother, or you may find her
in the doctor's office, beneath white jacket, the doctor.

The stranger woman, now a mother, a wife, or maybe
not even a wife or a mother, not a daughter, because

having left home, she's found no other fireplace
that will take in the son's wife as if she were

a daughter. Stranger woman, giving up mother,
father, sister, brother, all the smell of cooking

which having shaped her, has let her go. In a new
town with husband or in a new country, you may

find her on a road, following other people's dreams,
or maybe not even following other people's dreams.

THE WOMEN IN MY FAMILY

The women in my family were supposed
to be men. Heavy-body men, brawny
arms and legs, thick muscular chests and the heart,

smaller than a speck of dirt.
They come ready with muscle arms and legs,
big feet, big hands, big bones,

a temper that's hot enough to start World War Three.
We pride our tiny strings of beards
under left chins as if we had anything

to do with creating ourselves.
The women outnumber the men
in my Jabbeh family, leaving our fathers roaming

wild nights in search of baby-spitting concubines
to save the family name.
It is an abomination when there are no boy children.

At the birth of each one of us girls, a father sat prostrate
in the earth, in sackcloth and ash, wailing.

It is an abomination when there are no men
in the family, when mothers can't
bring forth boy children in my clan.

FOR KWAME NKRUMAH

When the news came that you had died, your sons
gathered in the front way, and did not know why

they gathered. Smoke in the fireplace curled upwards,
and the elders said how good it was that you'd left

so much smoke behind. When dawn comes, we need
the ash, we need the charred wood and chips of wood

to light the new fire. Every day needs its own fire since
no one borrows one night's moonlight for another night.

Kwame, Osagyefo, sharp eyes that saw the history we
now live. When you died, there we were. We gathered

to hear the sad news, and told our mute selves how strong
you had left us even though we knew how truly weak

we had become. Today we've burnt up all the shrines
you built, shrines of times to come; the vision we saw

in your eyes has perished with time. We cannot even find
our way back to where you stood, proclaiming that someday—

Africa would be free, one day, Africa would be truly one,
you said. Today, I saw our ancestral masks on sale here

in America, downtown Kalamazoo at the Black Arts Festival.
The very shrines, now doomed artifacts, something you

never told us about. That they would burn down everything
we had? That they would bring our own relics to stand

between us and the new world, just in case someone needs
to cover their immaculate wall? That we would buy

our own treasures from corner streets downtown America?
Your photo was downtown Kalamazoo too, on sale,

blown up by the artist who blows up other peoples' ancestors
for sale. They have brought back our masks, masks from

years and years ago, Kwame. A woman next to me fiddled
with the mask, turning it side to side. You could still see

the white chalk, white mud from ages of living in the shrines.
Other peoples' gods, other peoples' ancestral relics in

other peoples' land. If you could come and see the castles
you built, or see the sons you carved up the land for, Kwame,

who knows if you would laugh or cry or sigh or just stand
there while the rain pours down your face. Kwame, they

are making new books about you now. Your enemies
know how to tell your story better than your friends.

Lamentation after Fourteen Years

If you can sit beside the river long enough,
the tide will come in. You'll be there
for the river's rising—that urgent leaping
only a river can make.
You'll see how the coming tide departs,
leaving behind herring, catfish, *gbuga*,
snappers, where river meets swamp,
where swamp meets land, meeting you.

You'll see the crab or fish or lobsters or clams,
forgotten in the river's rush back to sea.
The poor used to wait on Monrovia's beaches
with bowls or baskets for the fishermen at sea.
Give-away catch can now feed a household.
Today we wait with straw baskets
and buckets, long lines,
we wait, all over the world, we wait;

not for *gbuga* fish or snails, not for the river's
refuse or the fisherman's *dash*—
Instead, we wait for peace, days of quiet,
ocean nights. They say, "if you set your eye
on the moon, you can see right through it."
So I clip away tree branches around my house,
from my front way, so when night finally
comes, I can sit under the sky
and watch the moon come home.

We do not long for yams or rice or oil. We do not
long for clothes or beds or babies; we sigh, not
for lack of tears or lack of laughter. We sit here,
my family and I, reliving the war—Charles Taylor's
cruel warfare haunts us like weeds left so long,
they eat up the yard. We sit here, God,
and we say, give us peace. We ask for

those quiet nights where only the Atlantic's
waves can roar. After so many years,
we long only for the end of war—
not for bread or beef; not for gin or rice,
not for roads or guns, not for street lights—
the sun comes out, and we say, God,
just give us the moon, the big blue moon.

BROKEN WORLD

To every winning team, many more will lose—
many defenders, goalies, linebackers, dribblers, attackers,

ball catchers, and now one lone, winning cup from which
no one will ever drink. To every war, there are no winners.

To every living, many more dead will go unmarked.
So many lives lined up for death; so much of what took

forever to build, goes up in some cloud. So many buried
alive or executed—a stray bullet, accidentally passing.

So many players who never knew the name of the game
they played, yet they played, without even knowing they

were playing until someone found them dead by the road-
side. Today, here are St. Louis Rams, walking away from

the Super Bowl, carrying the Super Trophy. Tennessee
watches with a tearful eye. But below the deep Atlantic

in Abidjan, a plane has just gone down. One hundred
and sixty-nine, gone down, and all this time, I was here

watching what Americans call "Super Bowl". I do not know
the game; it is not even my game to lose or win, but my

heart pounds hard for the game. Sometimes, I can feel
my skin slowly becoming American. Is life a game you can

win or lose? Will winning warlords ever know the extent
to which they have lost their war? How can anyone count

those who have won and those who have lost our war?
How can anyone travel from town to town, from country

to country, from refugee camp, to refugee camp, counting
our living? How could we dig up each shallow mass grave

for all the tens of thousands who were never counted?
Why should anyone want to count at all? Show me the trophies

of our war, so I will take you to a field, where all
the massacred still gather at night to bind open, bullet

wounds even though they are already dead. When warriors
come home from war, carrying on their hands, trophies

of booty, all the bullets from their weapons, gone, do
we ask them to show us their scars? The after-war *Dorklor*,

with all its drumming and dancing was never meant
to be merry—not even in their jubilation at victory.

You have only to watch the dancing warriors' feet to know.

V

Poems from:
BECOMING EBONY
SOUTHERN ILLINOIS UNIVERSITY PRESS, 2003

"A mother is a mother still,
The holiest thing alive."
—SAMUEL TAYLOR COLERIDGE

In the Beginning

In the beginning, there were women, and all things,
creeping and non-creeping, were good.

That was before time could tell daylight from night.
When men could speak women's tongues; before

the sea turned blue and took up rolling, foaming, like
a big glass of fresh palm wine. Before oceans learned

to rise and fall, before rivers were first named rivers.
Before they named the Cavalla River, *Cavalla,* after

the fish or the fish after the town, or the town after
the river. When Cape Palmas, where I come from,

became *Cape Palmas;* before there was even a cape
or palm trees. Before Cape Palmas began to give birth

to palm trees that sprouted with fat bottoms and began
to rise, and the coconut learned to be sister to the nut

palm and the nut palm to the bamboo palm, the bamboo
palm to the thatch; or when their grandfather made

them blood relations or straw relations or bamboo
relations or cabbage relations or long, thin leaves

relations, or whatever it is that makes them seem
identical twins. But bamboo knows how to prick my

finger when I touch it with an angry heart; the palm tree
will prick lightly, while the coconut stands there, tall.

Coconut breasts hanging from its chest, or head,
or whatever. The way a bamboo grove used to prick

our toes when Mudi and I wandered under its swampy
territory. That was before the time when women took

upon themselves to birth babies, even though men
knew how to, or before men went around boasting

of having this many children and this many sons upon
their mere fingers. *Iyeeh* says men really birthed babies

then, and women boasted of being the fathers of babies
then, and the children ran for their fathers like they do

today for their mothers when a father calls them for
whipping with a cane. That was long before the car road

bulldozed the giant walnut, the oak, chopping up
the towns and the forests into roads, and rubber trees

sprang up where the forests were, and the coffee
became a tree, becoming first cousin to the cocoa,

and the palm nuts went to the city to be sold for coins.
We girls grew wings like pepper birds—no, no, like

eagles, or like jet planes, and could fly or hop on a truck
to the city where streetlights cannot tell the villager

from the city dweller; where a man cannot tell his wife
from his lover; his *inside* children from his *outside*

children; where all have lost their hearts to the bars
and the dangling lights, and people fight on street corners;

and after all that, I and all the girls of the world learned
to run wild, too, like wild flowers—no, no, wild, like men.

All the women of the world becoming just men.

I Used to Own This Town

This place used to be my town… even when
the river rose from its own bed, taking up residence

with us in the rainy season, hiding under our beds
and dining tables; in kitchens, bathrooms, and

the town's pots and pans went sailing past us like
speed boats in the rain. Then we children splashed

about while our Mamas wept for mattresses
and pictures and all those memories floating away.

In the dry season, we ran in between houses, ponytails
and flat chests, panties or just bikinis, bare feet

and nappy hair, turning red from the dust and heat.
Then all the boys, in shorts, would dash with us

into Auntie Vic's big, black tub—until one day, I figured
out how to make her son, Mikey, breathe under

the tub full of water. All I wanted was to see how
a boy can breathe under water, and Mama comes

with rattan, giving me such a whipping… Slip Way,
loud Accra bars where Ghana High-Life-Beat

ran away with the night while we slept. Slip Way
was my town—where you could slip away, sit beside

the river and watch giant crabs and *gbuga* fish
swim around you. Up Crown Hill, no one guessed

we were hiding beneath that hill. Monrovia rushed
away without us. Did Monrovia know we owned

the river down there? Where the town humps like
a weary camel, we owned the hill, the sloping,

hanging rocks, clinging on tightly to the hill; we
owned the river, the fish and the kiss-meat shells.

The sun returned home at dusk, and we children
were running all over the place, hollering, and our

Mamas couldn't tell their own voices calling us home—
we were singing and laughing at how we could scare

a Mama out of her breath. And all the fathers coming
home, sweaty, oily faces, rough concrete hands.

At night, *Yana Boys* came home too, from Waterside
marketplaces—the bursting sewage coming back

to town, the smell of fish. We owned all the dust,
the rocky hills and all that poverty. So much laughing,

the giving and taking with everybody into everybody,
into everybody's business. When the moon came out

at night, we ran to the street, giggling. One long,
crooked line, marching, as the moon followed us.

GET OUT OF HERE, BOYS!

When we were children, we lived in Slip Way, Bishop
Brooks or Bassa Community, laid out, the masterpieces

of an unskilled artist. We were Turtur and Muriel and Mikey,
Comfort and Teeta, Sunday and me. Me, thin like a needle,

and my friend, Turtur, looking like she would break in half.
It was not just the houses matted into each other, not just their

zinc roofs touching, not just grass running from one door to
the other, too many pots boiling in one big kitchen. It was not

just us children in the rain, playing *Rain, Rain Come Down*,
or *Nafoot* or *I Was Passing By, My Auntie Called Me In*.

It was something, you see, just something. The boys running
around, shirtless. Little sticks for guns under skinny arms, in

between houses, chasing an enemy, playing *Cowboy War*;
but we girls, in our corners, bamboo sticks for people,

cardboard boxes for gates, playing *Family* —then the boys
came running, feet too big for shoes, barefoot, stomping over

our make-believe houses, our bamboo people. Sun so hot it
could set the whole world on fire, and there they were, shouting,

"Kpaw, kpaw, kpaw... *WAR*... ready?" "Yes, war ready!"
And all that shooting began, make-believe shooting, mashing

up our bamboo people in their bamboo beds. Then Auntie Vic
would shout, "Get out of here, boys!" Today, here we are, all

of us now women with husbands, men with wives and children,
living in London, Manchester, waiting on the war in Abidjan,

Accra, Kalamazoo, oh, Kalamazoo, Chicago, New York, Jersey
City. Now, Monrovia's on fire, kpaw, kpaw, kpaw. "Stop that

noise, boys, get out of here," Mama would scream when those
boys broke through her room, hiding right under Mama's bed.

BECOMING EBONY

for Mama

"Did I come all the way here, to hide from the sun?"
Mama would sigh. I can still see Mama standing

at the window, watching dark clouds, cold winds,
yellow leaves—November. Leaves from

my neighbor's yard arrive from yesterday's fall.
November rations its sunshine here in Michigan.

Today, I wish the end of clouds, the end of sky, the end
of windows—only curtains bright with daffodils,

African violets, hibiscus, wild thorny roses side by side.
I want to see the end of neighbors with falling maple

leaves, a lazy dog on a leash, barking at flying leaves.
Those who have no windows do not wait for the sun

to come in. Those who have no windows will not hear
my neighbor's dog. Here in my living room, the glass

window bends the sunlight; a dying fern leans. I am
a killer of plants seeking refuge in my living room.

I want to see the end of death. An ebony lion on my
glass table waits patiently for the sun, like Mama,

in Byron Center, waiting at the window for the sun
to come in, waiting for the war to end at home.

The day Mama died, I waited at the window to see
if the sun would come in, to see if my brother would

call again—the uncertainty of waiting so a moment will
undo itself, to undo that dreaded call, to undo death.

How many calls can undo death? An ebony carving
knows the uncertainty of skin, the uncertainty of time,

the uncertainty of waiting. Brown wood, darkening
slowly, becoming ebony all the way through.

The ebony at home knows how to unfurl wide, green
branches, how to die slowly, becoming woodwork,

a ritual mask for the harvest dance, an ebony lion,
perhaps, on a glass table. That familiar feel of carving

knife, the sharp cut, when the carver no longer recalls
his purpose. Crooked edges, polished by the artist's

rough hands, and then, what was wood becomes marble—
a raw tree trunk yielding its life until what was wood

becomes iron. The ebony knows how brief color is—
when sap licks itself dry into rough threads of wood.

They say after the sap is gone, then comes strength.
The ebony knows how final color is, how final death is.

All the Soft Things of Earth

All the soft things of earth sighed when my mother died.
All the quiet noises of this world stopped, at once.

Not even the drying, wet leaves, after fall had tossed
them so. Not even the robin that sits upon a twig

in my backyard knew what to say when my mother died.
Not even wet tears which death demands. All the soft

crevasses of this earth and of ground, sighed; the dent
crevasses of pavement after so many years. All the hands

that tremble at bewilderment, my hands lie helpless
and cold on my lap. When the wind blew past, it sighed

deep, like taking in deep breaths of air, a laboring,
as if the universe had just stopped. As if I had just died.

Requiem for Auntie

When the dead first arrive in death, their eyes stand
naked and wide and bare to the bone. This gaze

numbed my girl eyes the day they brought my Auntie
home. As the dead in the land of the living made a big

fuss to welcome her, I rushed out of bed in sleeping
gown, no slippers, into the parlor I ran behind my

father, carrying white sheets for her. Up the cold
dew-wet stairs, I ran. They are keeping her upstairs

in our unfinished upper floor, I thought, to wait
for the funeral car. I could feel the cold night

shadows creeping. My stepmother's muffled
sobs up there, something gone wrong, in the dark

where my father tiptoed, carrying white sheets
and the silence. There is no silence, I say, like

the silence of death, no loneliness that surpasses
the loneliness when your Auntie has left her body,

and the living are left searching for something to do.
Now the town lay halfway between sleep and death,

between Monrovia and the dark, meandering
of the Mesurado, whose tireless going and coming

leaves one empty of words, leaves the river banks
bereft. You can hear the Mesurado going to the ocean,

and then returning. That fruitless rushing of a river.
My Auntie, laid out upon a blue mattress in the parlor

of newly laid concrete tiles, a dim lamp burning
over her head. She must not feel the cold tiles against

her skin, I imagined, but we know that the dead cannot
feel, that their skin loses its feeling at the departure

of the soul. I watched my father's fruitless making
of the bed, laying his youngest sister down, though

wide-eyed, she stared. What is she looking at, I
wanted to ask someone. What is it that the dead see,

that the living cannot know? My father stood there like
a wet bird standing in the stillness of shallow water.

The mysteries of this world are not in the living.
The mysteries of this world are in the dead cold of

death, in the weathered things of this world, in
the silence that the dead refuse to take along when

the dead leave. I saw my stepmother rush to shut those
eyes, pressing closed my Auntie's eyelids. You could still see

the thin line where her eye-liner was now a birthmark.
My stepmother went from one leg to the other, stretching

my Auntie's legs, her still polished toenails, stretching
out my Auntie's arms. There used to be Sundays when

she had come walking down that road, bringing gifts
under her arms for us children, and we'd run to meet

her partway. Today, only a nylon gown shivered around
my skin, my teeth rattling. My stepmother stood now,

wiping the water running down her own cheeks, then
breaking out wailing loud, *po-po-wlee-oh*, the Grebo cry,

and yet I stood there, two o'clock, the neighborhood, asleep.
What if my Auntie had died at noon or at dusk, bringing

in the evening's hurried feet and cars, with Monrovia
hollering for her? Me, standing there, the cold dew

stairway, the sleeping houses, the swamp and the river—
so many real people at rest in an unreal country.

Today Is Already Too Much

The pigs are squealing now.
It is feeding time, and here, the younger
climb upon the older—the slob of grains
and chicken greens, rotten tomatoes
and clover grass will fatten them sadly.

The Mesurado's tide comes rushing in,
but the swamp hurriedly gulps down
all that salty water in mouthfuls—tomorrow
the river will return with
better fish and crab from the Atlantic.

Before the swamp, the hill heaves gulps of air,
breathing in today—who knows
if tomorrow will ever come.
My neighbor next door lives day to day,
to market today for bitter balls and rice,
again, to market, tomorrow.
Today, she says, is already too much.

There is wailing outside my backyard.
"Junior is drowned," I hear.
Junior has swallowed up the Mesurado
in huge gulps, and now, they are bringing in
my neighbor's boy with the afternoon tide.

I rush outdoors, barefoot down the hill.
You mean, that skinny, dark-skinned Junior
was gone fishing where the Mesurado
washes over quick swamp, quick sand?
My neighbor's boy, gulped down
all that swamp?

Right in the middle we form a circle where
death has stretched Junior out, on the ground
like a sheet. "Where did all that water settle,"
someone asked. The boy, flattened
by dark, quick swamp, not a drop
of water for all his thirst and hunger.

This Is What I Tell My Daughter

If my father hadn't scared me, I wouldn't be here.
I'd be somewhere down Jallah Town or Slip Way,
where the Mesurado dumps its junk by dark swamps.
I'd be carrying buckets full of dirt to turn
Monrovia's swamps into dry land. Or I'd be
somebody's wife, trying to be somebody's wife.
This is how I scare my daughter.

You wouldn't be here. You'd be somewhere,
where babies wait in long lines to be born,
little babies with sore feet, waiting
in the unborn world, where food can't grow.
I would have had ten children before you were born.
You, there, standing in line, waiting to be born,
while I'd be in some overcrowded town,
some unknown city or village, with skinny-
legged children, mucus noses, bare feet,

crying for food. I'd be there, one husband
each month, one room each month.
On Capital Bye Pass, where I grew up,
all the boys knew how to get a girl pregnant.
All sorts of men and boys, all sorts of people
lurking at windows, in doorways.
Plenty of men from Nigeria, from Sudan,
from faraway villages in Liberia, from Mars.
This is what I tell my daughter.

My father, a barbed-wire fence,
his needle-poking eyes, scaring boys away.
The boys called him "CIA chief."
The girls on Capital Bye Pass—with their perky,
brown cheeks, their smooth pretty skin,
their sophisticated steps.
My father called them *gronna-girls*,
bringing home sad trophies in teen arms.

M-T, Turning Thirteen

My son, M-T, comes home from school,
attached to two black wires, dangling,
his arms also dangling along those long legs.
M-T dances his way through our house,
through the street, through this world, and only
the rhythmic rocking and banging as his head
rocks and his lips move will tell you

M-T is still alive. His ears connected to wires
from a band around his head, into one pocket.
Tubes hanging down my son, M-T's body.
It is a thing to see, I say, my boy no longer
connected by an umbilical cord; instead,
it is just these plastic veins carrying sounds.
My son, now gathering reinforcement

for those civil war teenage years. At school,
they all walk the same, talk the same, laugh
the same, it is no use now—we've only
cloned ourselves. Now when he passes me in
the house, I conclude, like my mother, like
my Auntie, like my mother's mother's mother's
mother, we give up our children one by one;

I say, like a woman, after all is said and done,
giving up just when the baby is finally crowned,
and coming, the baby, the hero. Labor pains
will conquer us all just the same. We scream,
"I can't do it anymore—I can-not—push!"
My son, M-T, has just been admitted into
the world, where teenagers live.

The CD boom box booms; the stereo
is his keeper. His room shakes the window
panes; the walls bang the music out in steady
vibrations through the day. At night, my
neighbor shuts her windows tight, and I say,
she has just girls, you see, just girls.
So blessed, I say, *so miserably blessed.*

THESE ARE THE REASONS THE LIVING LIVE

Here come my children again, pushing chairs out,
in my way. They giggle, fall, and scream.
The family room leads into Ade's room
all littered with broken toys, old crayons, broken
only in the middle. Half-used paint, caked and cracked,
the treasures of a six-year-old.
These are the reasons the living live
and the dead decided to die.

My teenage daughter is laughing tonight.
You can write a poem on her foreface tonight—
let it linger in her eyes, hang a poem from a strand
of her thick, black hair.
To hold laughter in a line of a poem is like
capturing my daughter in a poem. It will be easier
to catch a bird with my left hand, easier to pull
out a lion's tooth, to hold a line of a poem down

to the level of Adam's wife. To let it linger in Eve's
serpent-flirting eyes, to the level of the song she sang
to the birds; Eden's serpent watching, its fins
licking the corners of a poisonous mouth.
Some days I thank my mother for bringing me here.
Some days I thank my children for keeping me here.
When I am ninety, before I die,
I'll count my children's toes and fingers again.
Will they still have legs and eyes and arms then?

For My Husband

We lived through rationed minutes at Soul Clinic
Mission displaced center, on rationed grains and fear,

and then night visited its shadows despite the odorous
air from the Killing Rubber Bush. One day I asked

if you were sure this was still Liberia. You looked
at me and said, "It's okay, my wife, it's okay."

Our children, ill, and starving, pleading for milk, for
a candy bar, for bread and meat, for a birthday gift

and cake, and we looked at each other and sighed,
knowing what children do not know. There were

no mirrors, no wardrobes, no saloons where we girls
knew how to spend a whole day, braiding or relaxing

long, dark hair, amidst the chattering room of girls,
working my long dark hair so I could let it loose

the way I used to let it loose. How I used to twist
and turn for you to see my new hairdo. Now with

no shaving blades or perfume soap, no perfumes
or nail polish, no iron or clothes to iron. Today you

looked at me, and said how beautiful I had become
in the war. And when the night came, we fell asleep

listening to shooting outside. You said you loved me
even though you saw what I did not see. And sitting

in the crowded camp, we held hands tight, waiting,
praying. I said I loved you while I saw what you did

not see. All the bones of our jaws and chests, piercing
through flabby flesh. We had become bones, eyes

and skin, but we did not know, and didn't wish to know.
I had lost my lipstick or couldn't recall if I had ever

had lipstick. And when we ate cooked green papayas
for potatoes, the heart of palm trees for meat, craw-craw

crabs for sea food, we shut our eyes tight, laughing
at ourselves. We were the lucky ones with no mirrors

in the war. Were we the lucky ones with eyes to see
the smoke, to see the missiles flying toward what used

to be home, breathing in air from the dead? We waited
to see if the food would kill us before the rebels could

kill us. We ate leaves we did not know we could eat;
we ate anyway, and lived through eating. We tried this

or that to see if we would not die eating this or that.
We made laughter we did not know we had. Did we

learn to sleep on cold floors, laughing at ourselves over
and over, our new eating habits, our new bathing habits,

our new songs, days handed to us in brief interrupted
installments? We were becoming new people, we told

ourselves. At night, we went to sleep knowing how far
away tomorrow was. Often, I looked to see if you'd

catch me smiling the way I caught you smiling.

They Want to Rise Up

In the unknown hours, when daylight is coming in,
and the dark gathers for departure,
when the winds stir pebbles along Liberia's shores,
you can hear the wailing.
From the coast of Harper to Sinoe, from Sinoe
to Bassa, from the coast of Bassa to Monrovia,
from Monrovia to Robertsport.

The ocean begins its soft whistling, like a new widow
that first morning after her loss.
All the dead at the ocean's bottom, whose bones
still search for refuge.
From the Atlantic's bed, a song rises in the ocean currents.
It is their sound that comes and goes, at dawn,
when the night is splintered into invisible bits.

ELEGY TO WEST POINT FISHERMEN

Your corrugated zinc shacks leaned into one another,
like a mask of crocodile scales, along

the fevered Atlantic, where waves wash away
white sand, tirelessly rising, falling, rolling, slapping.

We said your town would someday crumble
into this ocean; you'd die in the Mesurado,

just ahead. *One day these fishermen will all drown
in their sleep.* But you did not drown,

and your charcoal grills did not set your shacks ablaze...
you'd come too far to kill yourselves so ordinarily.

But one day the sand pulled you back as you tried to flee.
Before you'd had time to gather your fishing nets,

your canoes, waiting for the slap of water, your smokers,
ready to smoke *gbapleh* and snappers thin.

Will your bony fish graze these shanty skies smoky again?
Monrovia's skies exploded with jets, and you

exploded too, all of you, children, mothers, fathers,
fishermen, the smell of fish now your gravestones.

A Dirge for Charles Taylor

Charles Taylor sits like a wasted child
who has smashed the sacred bowl.
Firestarter of the hushed town,
Ghankay, the leopard
who came to town at harvest, eating
both the harvester and the harvest.
We will find our way back home by the imprints
of your bloody claws, *Ghankay*.
Banquet tickets to celebrate your dying
have sold out, but you will not die.
Plunderer, destroyer, do we delight
in your plundering or do we lament
abroad in other people's countries?
We have forgotten how
to sing the dirges you taught us to sing.
Those who die abroad now send their spirits
by boats, wading the deep waters at night
just to get back home.
Should we tell our children that there was
once Monrovia, sitting on a hill
where steel rocks breathed out hot vapors,
inhaling moist air? Should we tell our daughters
that there was a place where one could
put a shack down and stay alive on dry rice,
red palm oil and rumors?

AROUND THE MOUNTAINS

Sandy winds her car around little mountains
from Buffalo to Olean while we talk of husbands,

children, and the years. We're in a maze, these
Alleghenies humping, chasing one another up

and down. They will take you, if you please, until
the skies fall asleep in your eyes. Now I can see

how the hills lose us or how our eyes lose the hills,
giving up so the skies can take possession,

like a teacher of my child. Sandy says when
we get over the mountains, the sun will meet us

down below. Sometimes it is forever before we get
over the mountain, and the sun comes out

in trickling twilight. Sandy says when the trees
come out, this place is a paradise, but this year

the snow was forever falling. When the trees
come out, tell the trees, Sandy, to make the flowers

white and purple; to mourn the life, lost, the laughter
in Monrovia's streets, of people in the marketplaces

and on the long beaches; to mourn my neighbors
who wanted to know who you were, Sandy,

my American friend. Eleven years, and here we are,
chasing the Alleghenies, bargaining with these

hills and cops along roadside exits. Sandy says
she was afraid we'd all been killed, and I tell of how

a missile landed on our back porch, where Sandy
had stood, sparklers in hand, singing to America

on the Fourth of July; another missile bursting through
concrete walls, landing in the room where she

and Barbara used to sleep, the room my children
called Sandy and Barbara's room. I tell of leaving

home and refugee camp, of coming to America,
and Sandy sighs. But here I am, after eight years,

I'm going to St. Bonaventure to read poetry, where
Matt is Sandy's three-year-old, and Paul, her husband.

Paul, such a strong name for a husband, Sandy.
I'm going to read poetry where St. Bonaventure

University spreads itself thin on a field taken captive
by the Alleghenies, where students fall in love not

with the Alleghenies, as I have, but with each other.
I like my flowers spread out in colorful petals, a bed

under the skies. We know that spring is just
for a season. I like my husband warm, where summer

is eternal, when his eyes are laughing, and their pupils
fold under the milk in his eyes. I want to fold me

under my husband's arms, under his breath, the way
we did in the 1980s, before the war, before the children

came, before my strands of hair began to give way to
lost years, before the rebels came, before the soldiers,

before our years were ambushed into memory.

WHEN I MEET MOSES

Forty years, and already, the body is ready to go.
Knuckles ache, fingers fail you, and your eyes see things

that aren't even there. At night, your ears are like crickets
in your backyard, ringing in midnight before midnight.

When your joints crack, it's like an old door creaking
at dawn, when the baby's asleep, and you tell yourself,

"In the morning, I'll oil that creaking door; I'll oil
that door." All the hinges holding you together cry out,

it's time to leave now, although the party's just started.
Now, it's not just your teenage daughter disobeying.

When you were twenty, you were like a spring; the bright,
funny, long eye-lashed girl; face as smooth as a newborn's.

It was your big *tumba*, balanced hips and hairy legs
announcing your arrival, and all eyes turned. Now, see

all these signals each year brings—sagging flesh, painful
joints. Didn't we girls think our mothers would be the last

with aching knees? When I meet Moses, I'll let him say
how he lived over one hundred long years, already past

eighty before seeing the Burning Bush that I see every day.
Needing a cane only to stretch over some body of water

that splits in two, after going back and forth between God
and Pharaoh and those stubborn people below

that mountain. What kind of knees will carry a man, already
long past a hundred, up and down a mountain, carrying

the Ten Commandments engraved on stone? Now at forty,
why is my body in such a big hurry to be rid of me?

Coming Home to *Iyeeh*

I'm coming home so *Iyeeh* will die. So many years away,
and now, suitcases loaded with rolls of black cotton fabric,
matching earrings and hats. Second Mourning dresses
with lace trimmings at sleeves and collars, black and white
lilies running down all over. White laces at the hems
to bring out all that black.

This mourning must be properly done.

Some purple skirts and blouses, a purple dress to aid
in Second Mourning. I will need matching black shoes,
two-inch heels or just flats—even though I'm not one for flats
or rather, flats are not for me—*Iyeeh* will not want anyone
taking up her time and her funeral or wake-keeping uselessly
fretting over their own knees or joints, shoes or heels.

Every tear drop falling, every dirge sung, every wail or moan
or sigh… all the drumming and praise songs must be hers.
Iyeeh, Mother, *Khade-Wheh*, *Wahnjeh*, we praise you—
it is your children who now praise you… your wandering
stranger-children now coming home.
Where there are trumpets, they will sound.
We do not pour libation with ancestral hands or gourds.

They are the ones who drink libation… it is we who must pour.
All these years, the ground was parched and cracked.
Years of sun without rain or a bucket of water. I'm coming home
at last… the owl perches high at night, but the rooster sits low
on a cocoa branch. When the owl flies away at dawn
from the oak, it is the rooster, crowing, so the sun will rise.

The child that wanders comes home only to graves.

WE'VE DONE IT ALL

In my family, all the wars have been fought,
battles, won. All the losers have long settled
their losses in cattle or goats and sheep,
in women or farmlands or out of town.
Like *Bai* packing up, a tiny bundle under
now failing arms, leaving us even though
his eyes cannot see beyond a gaze. He's been
here so long, the Old Man no longer
needs eyes, no longer needs feet, no longer
needs us. Today, we watch him walk out
to *Borbor* Naapoh's farm when *Borbor* Tugba

says something he will not take; then again,
packing for *Borbor* Tugba's farm when
Borbor Naapoh says something he will not take.
In the dark night, just before bed when in
the rubber bush, you can hear crickets chipping
the evening into bits of darkness, fireflies
rush to bring him their own portable flashlights
as *Bai* stumbles out to leave, walking
miles of darkness to his younger son; or as
we look in the dark and see him hobble
into the house, out of the cold. As a child,

I wondered how old one gets before one loses
all fear of darkness, all fear of family feuds
or reasoning? How one sets one son loose just
to bind another. A distant cousin is sent away
for incest—whipped, peppered, and sent away from
Tugbakeh, where it is home to him, and never
again will be seen by family or friend
or that cousin he had raped.

WANDERING CHILD

"The child that wanders will not know her mother's grave."
—Grebo proverb

In my father's house it is payday, just before Christmas,
so the house bubbles full of unwelcome guests—

It is so long ago now—twenty years? Maybe, thirty.
There is beer, hot pepper soup and laughter.
Payday, my father is making payday talk.
In the kitchen, my father's wife, Ma Nmano, is cooking
goat meat soup with crushed tomatoes in a huge pot;
or we children are cooking the soup while
Ma sits there like the traffic police, pointing to this
or that as we rush around to give her what she needs.

Eight years ago at the airport, it is my own mother
standing there, wiping tears not just from the war.
She wipes one drop and then another while the plane
groans and waits so my family and I can flee home.
Ma Nmano is here too, wailing not just for my departure,
but also for TK, my foster brother.

TK who had promised her a nice bronze coffin, a long,
white gown to wear so when she met God, he'd know
she was Hne Nmano, *Sagba*, and nothing less.
TK and I would hold a great wake-keeping,
lots of food and lots of talk…
for our childless mother, and I'd sit there on *The Mat*
with my hair open, tearful, wailing,

a red mourning band around my head.
All the Grebo people would line up to shake my hand,
long faces; the women would sit close to me,
arms around my shoulders. Then on funeral day,
the Grebo band would arrive, playing,
"Na Nyebioh, Nyankeh Hne, Na Nyebioh."
Then we'd dance the way she used to dance during

those New Year's Day mornings when the bands
came with the new year to wake us.
New Year's Day, and we children ran out to the front
and rocked to Grebo rhythms. And all the last minute
fuss in the kitchen, whether to cook palm butter
in this huge pot or potato greens in that.
The women arguing among themselves over

how much pepper the wailing women would want,
and the kola-nut bowl there in the middle of it all;
people coming in, taking a bite of kola nut
and a pinch of hot spicy pepper. The beer and gin
and soft drinks passed around while TK
and my brother, Toh, ran up and down, checking on
the grave site, or whether there was enough

for everyone to eat and drink. Grand children
she never really had, running around playing *Nafoot*,
mimicking the wailing women on *The Mat*,
while the neighborhood filled with hundreds of wanted
and unwanted mourners. Family from all over would
come back home, sleeping everywhere in the house
because it was time to send Ma off. Instead,

one day rebels came for TK, shot him right there,
my father and Ma, pleading... Here I am, peeling eggplants.
My childhood follows me around where I slice
one eggplant after the other, to fry and steam cook.
I will cook make-believe Liberian torgborgee.
They say Africans want to have Africa in America,

pounding fufu to swallow, hunting for cow's feet in
Chicago, Detroit, New York. A hundred miles in search
of palm oil, gari, palm butter, sweet potato leaves.
Every alien wants to find home in other people's country.
After I fled the war, Ma died. One month, my father waited
for everyone who couldn't come to put *The Mat* down.

A POEM FOR MY FATHER

Pa wants another degree from me, a PhD,
for sure. Me, his oldest girl child who was supposed
to be a man. As if God won't let Pa into Heaven
without a family PhD. Won't listen to Pa's
old arguments about too many children plus too many
hungry relatives to feed. Too many *Mats* to put down,
and all those relatives from Kaluway arriving, red with
dust from two days' dusty highway. Heavy loads of palm
nuts, red palm oil, bags of cassavas, potatoes, eddoes…

all that rice, pounded so white, you can see right
through each grain. You see, we all know how that rice
was pounded just for each trip. Relatives, coming with dried
bush meat, smoked dry, like a rock. All those loads
of food, coming to our door at dawn, a truck's old engine,
beating leaded gasoline to help pollute our already
polluted earth. The cost of bringing all that foodstuff
through five hundred miles of rocky, hilly, country roads

of Grand Gedeh, Nimba, Bong… all this trouble for
nothing, since the loads are for some other relatives who
cannot afford to pay the truck driver's fare.
But Pa is the town's big book man—pays everyone's debt,
marries up everyone's daughter, and when they die,
Pa pays the gravedigger, the dirge singer, puts the bronze
on every casket, the black on every *lappa*, gin
for the mourning table, feeds the women on *The Mat*,
so the burial is merry, and the dead stand proud.

Pa buys the kola nuts to chew, meats up the soup,
so *The Mat* goes wild. That's why I'm back in school
after all these years. In all the homesickness and the snow,
Pa says, "Get that PhD before I die—
before they lay me in this earth." If I don't, the ground
beneath my feet will rock; my feet will slip and slide under
my father's turning over and over in his soggy grave.
The whole earth will open under my feet, a house
or two may tumble, rock, and fall… the ground,
opening its wide mouth to swallow me up.

MY NEIGHBORS' DOGS

All my neighbors have dogs, uncountable breeds
of dogs, little leashes around their dog necks.
My neighbors train their dogs to bark at dawn
like the rooster, to rouse the whole neighborhood
out of its sleep. In the evening when
I come home from work, these yelping,
howling, overweight dogs
welcome my car from the street
into my driveway. My next-door neighbor's dog
wants to tear down our wire fence. Giant claws
and teeth, its elephant body at the fence.
Someone needs to speak to that dog.
There are people in this world
who live on dogs, who will not understand
a dog in bed, a dog on a couch, a dog yelping.
There are places in this world where
kindhearted people eat dog at dinner.
But one neighbor keeps hers under
her comforter. Another ties her dog
to our shared fence, in the rain, in snow or sleet.

My neighbor has decided to keep her dog
chained to our fence, in case the gas meter reader
misses the meter, or the prowler comes in
while we're all gone. All my neighbors share
their dogs with me. That bark at two a.m.,
when all I need is sleep. My neighbor's
poodles are on water pills. They pee all night,
and my neighbor loves it that her little sweet
poodles keep us all awake.
At my backyard, I stand in my driveway
for my other neighbor's dog to bark until
it runs out of saliva. The dog wants to tear down
the wire fence that keeps us all apart;
our common fence with nothing common
between us, its invisible line keeping us
from knowing one another.
My neighbors' dogs are so kind.
One of these days, they may eat away our fence.

A Letter to My Brother Coming to America

for my brother, Norris Tweah

We just extended our daylight hours—so we can
shop the malls, pay our bills, shovel out snow,
take the garbage out. We still have twenty-four
hours in a day. I wash my own clothes,
cook my own meals, scrub my kitchen floor,
vacuum my house. Here, there are no maids
or houseboys, no long line of relatives

arriving at my door on Saturday mornings, needing
a few dollars for rice and fish, for a child's tuition.
Homesickness chips up my memories into cassava
pieces to fry at a street corner in Monrovia.

Our houses stand in silent rows here in Kalamazoo.
When I can almost hear the breeze pass, I wonder,
did a neighbor die, move away? Get a divorce?
Get married? Do they have children?
Do they not have children? Is my neighbor
white or black? Would my neighbors like me
if they knew my name? Do I have a neighbor?

Are they going to carve up your life too?

I wait at the window for the sunshine.
The pizza man will deliver my pizza, my only visitor
in months. I hear the bang when the postwoman comes.
Pull a curtain, and bang, she's gone. Of course,
my friends still say, "We're getting together, someday,
we're getting together." Dear Brother, did you hear me?

I used to hug people when I first came: a cashier at
the store, my next-door neighbor, the gas meter reader,
the girl down the street. I pulled on to sleeves,
keeping track of the homeless girl downtown.
And then, I settled. Are you still planning to join me?

My New Insurance Plan

My insurance company called me today—a great new plan
that's just right for me—thousands of dollars for me when

I'm already dead and gone, in the grave, while I lie still,
clasped in soil and water, beneath stones, and cold; my

husband or my children or Uncle Sam will claim this
benefit for me. But first, I have to die a certain way, in

a certain month, let's say, December or January, when
snow piles up along street corners and sidewalks, when

drivers can't get to work in their own cars. When cars go
sliding and crashing into walls. I must not die of AIDS

or pneumonia or chest pains; heart attacks will not satisfy
this great new plan. I have to crash on the expressway, into

a wall, a school building, into a house; I must die instantly
or they'll never pay. I cannot be hooked up to machines

or call in Jack Kevorkian; my insurance plan won't cover
such a procedure as Jack's, and the police can't arrive before

I swallow my last breath. My bones, all of my bones must
be broken, but my eyes must be in place. I cannot give up any

body parts before I'm safely in the grave. The cost, the soft,
pleading lady convinces is only a hundred dollars a month, a

bare hundred from my monthly paycheck, while I wait for my
car to come sliding on ice, seat belt strapped tightly around

me, buckled, of course; me, crashing into a welcoming wall.

The Corrupt Shall Rise Incorruptible

It's going to be something to see, right after
I'm dead and gone. Uncontrolled laughing down
the hall where my body lies in state,
and everyone turns to see if it's me getting up
to look over things, the way I have,
sending a peaceful room bubbling—
those secret enemies filing out so I can fill the room
with all my imperfection.

My three-week-old laundry out in some
dark closet, shoved there by my sister, Nanu,
who hates doing her own laundry anyway,
hates taking charge of things after anyone is dead.
All my friends looking so grim in this room
where silence has taken over without disturbing
a speck of dirt. All my loud laughing, now

immortalized, my fear of house cleaning,
immortalized; yelling at deaf children, over,
and done. And the dishes—let's get down
to the bottom of dirty dishes—palm oil stains glow
on imitation china; fufu, cooked before I died,
its residue, sticky, the way gum sticks
between the teeth of a grouchy Kru woman
awaiting her uncommitted lover's arrival
for the Christmas Eve dance.

Parched crust from rice cooked in my dying hour,
in the sink, exploding, as if to wail for me,
to mourn my passing, even though I almost never did
any dishes in my lifetime. Has grief so changed
the way of things that people actually think
I used to be clean?
It's going to be something to see—

my still naughty brother attempting to have
my dirty pots, laundry, and dusty carpet follow me
to the bottom of the grave. So when I rise
at the trumpet's last call, there will be chores for me

before I'm caught up in the air. And Jesus,
let's talk about Jesus, standing at the top
of Jacob's ladder.

That same ladder in Jacob's dream,
after he'd duped Esau out of Esau's birthright.
All that blessing just for one tasteless, spicy
bowl of alligator soup and palm oil on rice. Okay, maybe
not alligator soup, some soup, and Esau, the hungry fool,
Jacob, the trickster, now fleeing on foot,
Mama's boy, a rotten business—

that crooked business deal, still haunting us today.
Angels, descending, African angels, black wings,
climbing, descending, climbing,
and Jesus in a Total Involvement Suit,
long black beard, big, brown eyes, wide open arms,
telling me to move my bed into any house
here in Heaven.

Right down Nile Street in Heaven, I pick a house
where I sit, my palm under my chin, to worry
about my grandchildren not feeding their children well,
my great-grandchildren who cannot make up their beds.
My great-great-grand, not polite to an old woman
in the supermarket's aisles, not signing the cross
at the mention of my dear old name.

Jesus saying, "Forget the dishes, forget
the carpet cleaning and the dusting, forget
that your children must raise their own children,
forget the friends who haven't missed you all that much;
that the day you died, babies were born.
Forget that old woman in the supermarket aisles.
Forget that you forgot you are not God."

I Am Acquainted with Waiting

We waited to see if after all that smoke and shooting,
there was still us. Twelve years now,
all the anger subsiding, and again building up
among my countrymen who know how to go to war.

When Jesus hung there on the cross so many years
ago, waiting for the hour when all blood and life
would let go of him, Jesus, hanging on that cross,
his mother waiting below for the solitude hour?
Death came, comforting, like dew drops,
and then the resurrection.

After a woman has been laboring too many hours,
when the baby is finally crowned—
trust me, only the father stands jubilant at this time.
But when the waiting is done, after that last push,
after the tearing, and the baby's first cry,
when the sore mother holds her child

at her breast, trust me, how insignificant,
all that waiting. So I wait, you wait, we wait.
I am acquainted with waiting. I know the feeling
after all the flame and the smoke, after a long rainy night,
at dawn, the burnt shells of snails, the charred corpses
of scorpions, the forest fire, now quenched.
Trust me—we will return home someday, trust me.

VI

Poems from:
BEFORE THE PALM COULD BLOOM:
Poems of Africa
NEW ISSUES PRESS, 1998

Home is not where we live; home is where we belong
— AFRICAN PROVERB

Africa

The calabash
now shattered

her contents
spilled
like palm wine

across the regions
of the world.

TUGBAKEH: A SONG

A ripened breadnut hits the ground
at the outskirts of town.
Tugbakeh boys, half-clothed, run, a game.
Who will be the first to find
its smashed fruit, one of its kind?
Seeds scattered beneath the intermingling
of giant mango, banana, and orange trees.

War dancers in raffia skirts
jingling belled ankles, stamping
village dust in the dusky December day.
Dorklor is so hard to dance
when veteran dancers are in the lead.
Gbor-belloh, too, here he comes,
red rock chalks and charcoal paint
pasted onto his cheeks; his face, a scary mask.
He pulls out his tongue,
stretching it into a mile about himself.
Only the aged can explain
as onlookers run indoors.

The Dodo flaps her wings,
her song for the young that were just hatched.
The white doves will come home for Christmas
to hear her young sing.

Elders, chewing red kola nut,
laugh loudly; proverbs are talking
under the cotton tree. Sipping palm wine
as drums rock the ground
in an earthquake of festivals
older than the earth.
Trumpets follow.

Then come the town's women, renowned.
Years buried under hanging eyelids.
Feet, slapping graciously the ground.
Hips rocking in defiance
of age, arms swinging.

These *Bor-juo-eh* dancers' feet
dance life into this soil.

Kwee will come to town today,
before the *Town Crier* calls home
the night.
When *Kwee* begins singing,
near the outskirts of town,
Kwa-jah-lea will sound.
Women and children will run for doors.
Doors will be latched
when *Kwee* makes his way here.
The old men and the young men
will find laughter again.
Women will be born, will grow breasts
and find men. Will birth babies
for men, then find age when teeth fall out.
Women will lean lightly against their canes
and go gracefully to dark graves
never setting eye upon *Kwee*.

The Dodo flaps her wings,
her song for the young that just learned to fly.
Some day they will fly away
and join the chorus of dodo songs.

Drum pounders sit in that line
at *Tuwah-Kai*, under the baobab tree, pounding.
Short drums, tall drums, drums with wide bottoms,
long-legged drums, patient drums. Pounders sweat
as though they are the ones pounded.
Village children run screaming, chanting,
following dancers, overtaken by their dance.

*   *   *

Now Tugbakeh, like a stillborn, stilled.
No arguments for those slapping life
into its wrinkled bottom.
The breadnut still falls, though, and the breadfruit too.
The cocoa and mangoes are full, fruit falling,
smashed, piling under overgrown brushes,
abandoned in the sudden rush of war.

Kola nuts are full now, ripened
by empty suns, half-moons, years.
And the coconut trees now touch the skies.
On the ground, dried coconuts
are sprouting everywhere.
Every now and then a mango hits the ground.
Worms and groundhogs have much to eat.
Palm branches still wave, though,
and the wind blows from Tugbakeh's hills.
The forest has taken the streets
from us who used to own the forest.

The Dodo flaps her wings,
her dirge for the young that were not hatched.
An owl on the cotton tree branch
rolls its coconut eyes.

Where did the village folk go?
The elders who used to drag their long *Khaflahs*
on red, dusty Grebo ground
in the harvest drumming?
Where did the women go?
Their heads that could balance
a pail of water while their arms
swung, or held on to infants falling
out, the *lappa's* grip on their backs.
Where are the young girls who held time
in the folding of their palms?
Chalked cheeks, painted for village boys to see.
Eyes with long, bushy lashes.
Careless girls; polished faces.

Child Soldier

1.
Child of Liberia, Kahieh,
murdered in Harper
while your dreams bloomed, afresh
at midday.
Just before the palm could bloom;
before the bamboo shoot could spring out.
The brushfire set your branches ablaze.
The palm branch sprang out,
but the fire threatened in the brush—
palm nuts burning in Pleebo
so the planting season
will bring us a great harvest.
The palm branches caught in the brushfire.
Kernels still white, their tender shells, burning.
Gbolobo's tropics lending its young
so warriors will reap
crops they did not plant.

2.
Child of Liberia, Saye,
in Buotuo, you went
with doubting feet
that swayed to the rocking that broke
the dancers' feet.
Running, orphaned early,
where Tapeta takes us to the Gbi forest.
Child soldier, cutting the rope
that ties us to oak branches; branches
to trunks. These oaks
without which history is lost.

3.
Ghapu, Liberia's green palm,
you came from Bassa, trampling the coastline,
carrying adjustable ammunition
in our adjustable age.
I followed your footprints
along Sinoe's beaches, searching to know you.
Child soldier, called to war,

slashing your fathers, cutting off the root
that brings us water from riverbanks;
this root that calls the Cestos to the Atlantic.
Wlemunga, child warrior,
you for whom history waits
so we can end our anger.
You fell and fell until all lay silent
and bare.
Dying with eyes awake.
History will want to know.
History will want to know.

4.
Child of war, Kortu, my child
who followed where the road led
so crookedly from Nimba to Cape Mount.
From Ganta to Monrovia's rocky hills,
trampling the Mesurado swamps.
Your feet dug deep, printing
stories along Monrovia's hillsides.
Too early beckoned,
you followed too hastily
to grave mounds of dead warriors
in Firestone rubber bush.
Graveyards followed your footprints.
Gravestones, invisible to the passerby.
Our war children,
who follow men who have lost all reason.
Our war
that will not yield to the cries
of newborns, abandoned.

5.
This, my child, my Kahien,
called by our warlords—
our punishment for sins past—
who came demanding our sons
while we still carried them in young wombs.
Our sons, called by our war heroes,
blinded by gun dust, calling
for more children

though we were quickly made barren by battle.
Calling out for you, Kahien,
a sacrifice to gods who seek
more blood at the hand of more blood.

6.
My child, your nostrils
still full of early dawn mucus,
wetting your pants and bleeding,
wetting Liberia with your bleeding.
The adjustable automatic guns, handed you
at the killing of your father.
Our sons, our history made adjustable
in this adjustable age where
reason loses ground to insanity.
Child soldiers, our children.
Saye, Ghapu, Kahieh, Nimley, Kortu, Wlemunga...

WARRIOR

I am Tagbe-Toe,
come home from war.
But the kola nut tree
dropped its flowers
during the storms.
There are no greetings,
and I'm left at the doorpost
by my own clansmen.

The women are gathered
at the backyard
with water-filled kola-nut bowls.
But there are no kola nuts
for this spicy pepper
in earthen jars.
And here I sit alone
at the door post,
smelling its pungent odor.

Gbolobo has given in
to government troops;
our warriors' heads
crushed with guns.
Their brains thrown into the Gbi forest
to fertilize the land
so Tubman may some day
sell our timber.

There is no war song;
no drums to sound
a warrior's return.
But will the kola nut
not greet me
in my own town?

If I were *Yarkpawollo*
I would climb a palm tree,
a gun at my shoulder,
pointed at the innocent, too.
But mine is just a quiet homecoming
as I await my greetings
at the doorpost.

In Memory of Cousin Hazel: A Dirge
December 1988

Come and see me
who has buried herself.
Death has been cruel to me
from my youth.
And now that I am gray
I have dug into this red earth
and laid my navel string
into a hole so deep.

When the cock crows
I feel myself stirring
under the red earth.
My only girl is laid to rest,
and here I stand, wailing
over the hole
that has swallowed
my heart away.

My girl has gone
and done
what a woman doesn't do.
Has let her breath slip
while she brought forth life.
Our people say,
"One doesn't die in childbirth."
So now my child
will never come to town again
to roll my *Mat* away.

HERITAGE

My home is *Nganlun*;
sparkling *Nganlun*, emptying
its wealth of fisheries into *Sehn*, singing,
flowing between rocks and hills.
Nganlun, that caused the wanderer to stay,
the traveler to make home here in Tugbakeh.
Our thirst quencher, life giver, rushing
as if beckoned by a sacred call.
Nganlun runs in my blood,
between joints, and in my tissues,
flowing freely in my heart,
pumping blood to my brain and vessels.

Tugbakeh, that's home!
Where our family rope entangles us
in a spider's web, where we love and fight,
bending the *Toebo* family tree during
heavy family storms.
My father's father, and his father's father's father,
Bai Toe, called you home, this Tugbakeh
of aged trees in the red earth
looming over the narrow road
that leads to Harper.

My name is Jabbeh. *Jabbeh Cho*,
in a forest, hunting, the tornado mistook him
for a bunch of palm nuts, saved him
amidst the howling in the trees.
In me, he turned up dark, me, ebony,
after an endless line of *Toebos*
had passed on.
This long string of *Toebos*, on various rocky routes.
At a dead-end in us women.
But in our brothers, the branching roots.

Monrovia Women

Monrovia women...
Here they come!
You see their colorful faces
before you know their hearts.
Shining, red lips, red cheeks,
painted eyelids and lashes.
Perhaps they would like
to paint their pupils too!
Their eyebrows take to various routes
to suit their longing hearts.

Aye, Monrovia women...
Look at their necks!
You could build a mansion
from jewelry a single woman wears.
Sometimes, like Indians,
their noses wear gold rings,
while their ears themselves
wear several others too.

You have yet to see their hands...
Long nails painted
to match the various hues
their eyes and cheeks wear.
Fingers held apart
by heavy gold rings.
Oh, you should see them
walking down the road.

Monrovia women...
In evening gowns and dresses,
lappa suits and costly coats,
on their way to work.
You should see them at work!
They nurse and paint their nails all day,
and guide their skirts from hooking
on to a rusty nail.

Monrovia women…
Strolling in the humid sun
in high, expensive shoes.
If you would stop
to ask their toes
how much fun it really is,
walking in such heels,
I'm sure you'd say *aye-yah*,
for our poor Monrovia woman.

I'm Still Thinking...

Today I prayed for you to die
in the July downpour, the rain
beating down aluminum zinc roofs,
into gutters, turning red
upon muddy hillsides. You, drowned
in the St. Paul River. Rain water
from Monrovia's hills will meet you
at the arteries of St. Paul.
Waves washing you up and down
like children playing seesaw.

Divers won't find you, but
the gigantic sea crabs will. They'll snip
your toes, one by one, then your fingers—
your Ma, sitting on *The Mat*, waiting, hoping.
And those divers, arriving each day, heads bowed,
they'll say, "We didn't find his body."

Oh, no, God, don't let him die that way.

Today I prayed you'll just drop and die.
They'll lay you up like a real corpse.
You've always been a corpse. You, Dave,
stretched out like an ironed gown
in a wooden box painted black with tar.
Face wrinkled from cheating on us girls.
Flies everywhere, singing, and we girls standing
at a distance in high-heeled shoes,
silky, pink blouses, sweet perfumed hair, and
laughing loudly.

Oh, no, God, don't let him die that way.

You kept me standing, Dave, waiting.
Lace trimmings running down
my wedding gown, me waiting. Eternally.
I still wait at weddings, Dave, for you.

Lord, let him live, waiting on death.

You will rot, waiting on women. Your wife
will dish you up on a plastic platter to eat,
your yelling wife, a beast, cooking you
half-cooked meals.
Birthing you half-hearted babies, beating you up
with a leg from your dining table.

You'll meet me and my husband, a real man,
down Randall Street. You, standing there,
wrinkled with age.
Oh no, God, don't let him live that way.

I pray, today, wait a minute God, I'm still thinking.

OUTSIDE CHILD

Her husband comes home, bringing in
this roll of blanket, arms around it, a ball.
Red fingers poking out, reaching.
What is that? She says. This man,
immobile; feet upon marble floor, and
the sunlight here, finding its way through

windows; rays dancing, curtains swaying
to the Atlantic breeze that visits Sinkor
at sunset. She takes this bundle,
peeps into its pink face; cheeks, puffy and red,
a pyramid of a head,
brown eyes, brown lashes, no hair, a human?

She unwraps it like a silly child
opening a long-desired birthday gift, fearful
of what it contains.
This wiggling thing, a child, a boy child, screaming?
Is he motherless? She holds him to her breast.
This thing that will rob her of heart and mind.

Her husband stands like a tree
after lightning has struck. Lips glued
onto teeth, tears streaming down wrinkled
cheeks, arms wide, begging.
But for what?
She stands there, hugging this child,
talking to this stranger in a blanket.

My child, he tells her; this man,
bringing her a child like this from the outside?
After long nights, loud bars, gin,
whisky, beer cans, and women?

Her oven heart, her furnace.
This man comes bestowing a child upon her?
Is this what I win? She asks.
Having cooked him spicy torgborgee,
kpassajama, okra, stewed with shrimp,

pigs' feet, smoked salmon,
bush hog-meat, bony fish, wild chicken legs?
Poured upon fluffy rice, fufu,
cassava steamed to taste?
For fixing him up during the flu or
malaria evenings? Giving him babies?
Putting up with his family, uncountable

in numbers and ways?
Her husband brings in this alien thing?
Where is his mother? She screams.
But he stands there, watching curtains
around them dance.
Answer me, where is she?

ONE OF THESE DAYS

One of these days
there will be rejoicing
all over the place.
There will be so much shouting,
so much wailing,
so much dancing.
There's going to be
such dancing
as we've never before seen
in Monrovia.
There's going to be a day
like that, I say,
and there's no one
who will be able to stop us.

I'm going to train
my feet
for that day.
It's going to be something
in Monrovia's streets,
all potted up with
bullet holes.
Our feet tapping will make
all those holes
vanish just like that,
before we know it.
I can't wait to see the faces
of those who have defied
death all these years.
Man,
I just can't wait.
All those who died
eating

those hot, burning bullets
and all our families
gone, will want us
dancing
and singing again.
Man, I just can't wait.

Where will all those soldiers be
when our drums
break through the air?
You mean
all those villages
laid bare by bullets?
Those cities, flattened
by their rockets?
Man,
it's going to be something!

All of us refugees
will come home again;
and we will cook
on twenty-sixth day again.
Palm butter and rice,
potato greens in one pot,
dried fish, spiced,
the other,
with cassava leaf in red oil.
Old time kpassajama! My!
We will steam jollof rice,
fufu, paddled with fufu sticks,
dumb-boy, pounded hard
in flat mortals again.
The soup, oh Man!
We will eat like the good old days.

I bet
the old people
will put *The Mat* down.
The elders
will shout, "—*Ba-te-oh*,"
"*Ba*"
about the pot
that was not broken.
Some old women will wail,
or sing a dirge
for those fallen
in this war.

Some orphans
will go out, searching
for those lost loved ones,
hoping they are alive.
Some of us may weep.
Sometimes,
tears can heal.
But Man,
after all the wailing
there's got to be some laughter
with the tears.

Com' on,
get ready for the dancing
and hollering
in the streets of Monrovia.
Man, Monrovia, we're coming.
We will dance,
and dance down Waterside
with all its rocky hills and traffic.

Its crowded market stalls,
heavy Big Mamas, *gronna* boys and thieves.
All its corrugated zinc shacks,
Waterside life.
I'm waiting until
they put this wildfire out.
Sometimes, I just can't wait
to put my feet to the test.
Who can say the kind of dancing
when this flame
is out, oh, Man!

When I Get to Heaven

When I get to heaven
I'm going to shout hallelujah all over the place.
Dancing the *Dorklor*, the *Wahyee*,
the Ballet, the Rock and Roll.
I'll dance the Brake, the Rap, Hip Hop.
All the dances only sinners have danced.
I'll sing Opera, the African way,
dance the Ballet the African way.

When I get to heaven
I'll pray so loud, shaking hands the White way,
the Black way; greeting with kola nuts
as the Grebos do.
I'll lie prostrate, to greet
the Yoruba way. Snap fingers to greet
as Liberians do.
There will be no boundaries, no laws, no rules.

When I get to heaven
I'll sing the blues and dance the *Sumu*.
I'll paint my face with white chalk and red rock,
sit with missionaries so all can see.
I'll pound my drums, shaking my *Sahsah*.
Blowing my trumpet the African way.
Dancing to Jesus the African way.

MINORITY

At home,
I am a Jabbeh, *Jabbeh Cho,*
married to *Seo Paton,* now a Wesley.
A *Toebo,* from *Gbaplepoe Paton,*
Chee Dawanyeno, Jlajeh. Bodior line.
A Tuo, from Tugbakeh, of Wyne lineage,
where the Jabbehs have their place
in the history of the Grebo people.
I am Grebo,
the Grebos, coming down
the Grebo Forest, seeking the coastline.
The Grebos of the Gbolobo War,
the Grebo Wars
against Americo-Liberian dominion.

At home,
I am not only Grebo.
A Marylander of Marylanders.
I have never before
stumbled my way
into history.
I come from where
the Atlantic refuses to sleep.
Where the forest never turns yellow.
Where the waters run wild, cold.
Where the brooks sing a melody
to the sea.
Where the Cavalla rushes to greet
the ocean with kola nuts
and spiced pepper.
Maryland, where Cape Palmas
borrows land to the sea,
stretching its arm
to greet the sea.

I am Kwa,
A Kwa of Kwas,
where the Krus, the Grebos,
the Krahns, the Sapos,
the Bassas and the Belles
come from a common shoot.
We are a people
of all peoples.
Our lines run deep,
deeper than the soil
that meets the waters across West Africa.
In Africa, I am Liberian.
When I speak, I give myself away,
a Liberian.

I am African,
West African,
of Songhai, Mali, and Ghana,
a huge history, smeared with blood,
the blood of slavery.
We are Cain of Africa.
The sons of Jacob.
Having sold our kin to Egypt,
we've come to meet them.
Yes, they are our kin.
They look like us.
They even dance like us,
and laugh like us
and cry like us.
So America puts us together
in America's jar, a tight jar.
Minority.
Ah, what a word!

HOMECOMING

1.

I don't want to be a stranger
when I come home.
Yes, I'm a wanderer,
a woman.
But I don't want to be a stranger
in my hometown.
I will not stand outdoors
waiting in the dark
at the doorpost
of my father's house.
I want the fireplace lit.
I want the wood sparkling
with fire balls
when I come home.

2.

I want my kola nuts
handed to me
on earthen platters;
the pepper in earthen jars
spiced, like we know it,
when I come home.
Let them fetch me water
in white pails
from *Nganlun.*
Oh, the coolness of *Nganlun,*
sweet *Nganlun,*
that penetrates the heart.
Nganlun,
that never dries up
in the scorching heat of March.

3.
I don't want to stay
the wanderer.
I want my brothers
to take me in.
Let them meet me
at the gateway
of Toe Wyne's compound.
Let them bow
where libation
would have been poured.
Let them raise hands
to God
for sparing some of us.
When I come home,
I want to be treated
to welcoming songs of praise.
Do not forget my names.
I want my praise names
recited to incessant drumming.
List my names
in their proper order
like our mothers sang them
when we pestled rice
in wobbling mortars.
Remember our ancestors
for their deeds,
and let their names
grace those songs of praise
in my homecoming.

4.
If they kill all our brothers
who will meet me
when I come home
after this wandering?
Who will keep the wood burning
in our fathers' house?
You see, I am a woman,
the wanderer
made even more so

by war.
When I come home
to my people
I want to see my brothers,
all the sons of *Taabah,*
the greatest of our wanderers,
our mother.
I want her stock
lined up to meet
the new wanderer.
Our fathers gave us brothers
to keep the hut warm,
to keep the family smoke
rising above our roofs
so we can come home.
I am only a woman;
let my brothers live.
Let me come home
again.

Glossary

Alfred Musa Hill	An area in Paynesville City named after one of Charles Taylor's Commandos who reigned over a very murderous checkpoint, a place where hundreds of refugees lost their lives during the Liberian civil war.
Ancestral Stool	According to African mythology, a stool that the Ancestor patriarch sits on in the afterlife.
Bai	A Grebo word for father, uncle, grand-father or simply, elderly man.
Bati-Oh-Bati	The Grebo call or shout to order during the council meeting of elders.
Bati	The group response to the call during council meetings.
Bodior	The High Priest or spiritual head of a Grebo town. He is head of the Tuwah Kai, or holy house, where the shrine and religious relics are kept.
Borbor	A Grebo word for big brother, uncle, male cousin, or male relative.
Bor-juo-eh or Boh, Borh	A dance among the Grebo people of Liberia, usually performed by women during the dance of Kahn or Wlee.
Cho	The color red, but in describing some-one, it means light skinned.
Dorklor	Is a dance associated with the Wlee or Kahn (depending on which area of the Grebo tradition one is speaking of). Otherwise known as the War Dance, this dance is performed by men and women to celebrate victory after war, commemorate death, war, and many other significant occasions such as the honoring of great personalities. There are many dances around Africa, espe-cially West Africa, which are similar to the Dorklor.
Gbaliahde	Refers to the high forestland, and in my hometown, this meant the farthest

forestland, where the Jabbeh family land bordered Hanugbeh, another town, land that was constantly in dispute as our family fought to retain ownership. The term referred to something that means "far into the forest."

Gbaplepoe Paton

Two words: "Gbaplepoe" is a clan linage in Grebo country, like Seo and other clans. "Paton" means clan or family where one comes from.

Gbolobo

Is a town in Maryland County, west of Harper, its capital city. This town is noted for the Gbolobo War with the Liberian government in the 1900s during the Kru (Klao) resistance. My father's father, Bai Jabbeh, fought in that war, and taught me all I know about the Gbolobo War against Barclay.

Gborbelloh

The professionally trained magician (artist) and seer who is the official designated performer, working varying supernatural signs during festivities. He may perform strange wonders under the watchful eyes of hundreds of villagers.

Grebo (Glebo)

Is an ethnic people, linguistic and cultural group of Liberia whose main homeland is Maryland County, in South Eastern Liberia. The Grebos who migrated into this region of Liberia hundreds of years ago also inhabit parts of Grand Kru County and lower Grand Gedeh County as well as parts of the Ivory Coast along the Cavalla River. The Grebo Language is of the Kwa family of languages.

Harmattan

The cold/dry air that blows across West Africa, from the Sahara Desert.

Iyeeh

The Grebo word, like "Bai" for grandfather, "Iyeeh" is the name for grandmother or Mother, used to describe an elderly woman. Iyeeh in my poetry means more than this. Most often, I refer to my maternal grandmother, who was the greatest and first female influence in my life, a strong-willed woman, who, though a villager, was a feminist in many respects and shaped my thinking since childhood. She and my mother raised me until I was seven when my mother moved to Monrovia, away from her. And later in my early years, between eleven and fourteen, she was important in my life once more during my years in boarding school. She was a very independent, strong woman who my elders now say shaped my personality as a woman. She was married to a blind man, my grandfather, all her life from her youth, and therefore, was forced to be independent. The word, "Iyeeh" here in my works, refers to a powerful, spiritual force in my life.

Kahn or Wlee

Is the most significant ritual dance among the Grebo ethnic peoples. It is known as the War Dance because hundreds of years ago this was the dance performed before warriors went to battle and after. In modern times, this dance is performed to commemorate a significant birth, death, harvest, marriage, etc. Nowadays, the War Dance is performed even in cities.

Khade-Wheh

A Grebo praise name that means head wife, the main wife of the household, but also means big woman, great woman, the great woman, the queen of her household, a Grebo praise name used to describe a great woman, a girl, etc. It also describes what hierarchy is in a polygamous Grebo marriage, where the head wife is boss of the home.

Klahn-Klahn-Teh

Is the sound of the wailing, talking drum, the largest and tallest drum in a Grebo town or village. At the pounding, people from hundreds of miles away may hear and follow the sound to find out why the drum is sounding in a town. The meaning of the sound carries the message that there is grave news. "Klahn-Klahn-Teh" means "Grave-grave news."

Kru	An ethnic, linguistic, cultural group in Liberia whose main homeland is Sinoe County. The Kru, however, can be found in other counties like Grand Kru and other parts of southeastern Liberia. They are a family of the Klao or Kra linguistic groups, similar in culture to the Grebos, Krahns, Bassas, and the Belleh, having descended from the same Klao ethnicity.
Kwa-jah-lea	Is the call to a Grebo village in parts of Grebo country where Kwee, a male fraternity organization is practiced, a society of initiated men and young boys that excludes women, and therefore, when Kwa-jah-lea sounds in the outskirts of the village, no matter what a woman or non-initiates are doing, they must abandon it and move indoors, lock the doors to make way for the Kwee (the spiritual head of the Kwee society) to take over the town. The organization also performs public services like clearing the town, constructing roads, etc. for the town. These practices have been hit by the civil war.
Kwee	The spiritual leader of the Kwee society as well as the name of the fraternity of males who exclusively control the organization in a Grebo village, excluding participation by women. This is a fraternity among Grebos in certain areas West of Pleebo, Maryland County.
Koo-oo-koo-oh	A praise name that is rooted in my maternal mother's heritage. She called my mother by this name, and my mother called me by the name because it was passed on by Iyeeh. The call is a whisper or a call.
Lappa	The wraparound or skirt that is worn by most African women, and particularly, in West Africa. The lappa is now made more modern for the professional modern woman, turned into a skirt for more comfort and easy movements and dressing.

Na Nyebioh, Nyankeh Hne, Na Nyebioh	Translates to "My husband, Nyankeh Hne, my husband," and lyrics are taken from a popular and classical Grebo love song.
Nehwordeh	A Grebo word that means "Women of the Family," and only those who are genetically related by blood are Nehwordeh of any group. They are the female power of the Grebo clan, and are important in decisions in the family.
November 12, 1985	Refers to a very bloody time in Liberia's history, a day when defeated Liberian general, Thomas Quiwonkpa staged a failed coup on November 12, 1985 to overthrow Liberia's military turned civilian leader, Samuel K. Doe. The November 12 coup failed hours later, and President Samuel K. Doe's troops stormed the capital after retaking the government, and on the president's order, hundreds of people in Monrovia's streets and neighborhoods were massacred. General Quiwonkpa was captured and killed seven days later.
Nyene-Wheh or Nyonoh-Wheh	A praise name in Grebo that means "Great woman," and similar to Khade-wheh, but Nyene or Nyonon, which means "woman," when combined with the word, "Wheh," as Nyene-wheh or Nyono-wheh means "Great woman," and when combined with "Khade" as "Khade-wheh" means "Great wife," Great mother of the home, Great headwife," since Khade means mother of the house.
Po-po-wlee, popowle-oh	The classical Grebo chant and dirge that is hundreds of years old, from the beginning of the Grebo people, a cry, wail, call, that is another kind of messenger of grave news. The chant is a call to the town and the people to come and mourn for a tragic event. It is a dirge that women cry out to begin wailing for the dead or for horrible news.

Reburial or "Laying of the Plank"	Within a year of the death of a Grebo elder or statesperson, townswoman, or a person, the family, including the larger family, clansmen, etc. must carry out a major ceremony of celebrations, feasting to commemorate the dead person's entry into the ancestral world, a time, when they spiritually send the dead off to take their place in the ancestral world. Their reception by the dead depends on how well they are sent off. The feast and celebrations include all the Grebo festivities of Wlee, dances, singing, lots of liquor and food and a gathering of various towns and the hometown of the dead is crowded by guests, depending on how renowned they were. The Reburial is so important to the tribe, it is not unusual for the dying to preplan their Reburial rites and ceremony with their eldest sons even before they die. It is a violation not to send off the spirit, and Grebo mythology teaches that such a spirit remains in the world of the living, wandering, and torturing the family to do what is required of tradition.
Sagba or Sagba-Nyene	Grebo praise names and was my stepmother's praise name.
Second Mourning	A time of mourning in Liberia and among the Grebo, in black and white instead of in pure black, preferably three to six months after the first mourning in pure black.
Soul Clinic Refugee Camp	A boarding school facility where my family and I took refuge in the first Liberian civil war of a long series of wars that lasted fourteen years. This was one of the most violent and cruelest strongholds of the Taylor war, a place that saw the massacre and torture of tens of thousands during the war.

The Mat	A large mat or several mats, which according to Grebo tradition, is spread out and mourners sit and wail for a week or two to celebrate and mourn the dead. Every death in Grebo tradition requires The Mat ceremony with The Mat itself representing a symbolic place to empty all grief prior to the long burial ceremony.
Town Crier	An official of the town who is appointed or elected to be the public announcer, whether through the blowing of horn and a call, informing the town of grave or important news about their welfare. Decades ago, a Town Crier could even call out someone who committed marital infidelity, rape, etc. through a call to meeting, announcing the agenda of the event. His authority was based on information from the kingdom, the chiefs and elders of the town.
Tuwah-Kai	The important official council house in the Grebo village among certain Grebo people, my people.
Yarkpawollo	Yarkpawollo was a sort of hero in Liberia or a defect, according to the Liberian gov. in the 1960s of President William V. S. Tubman era when his presidency was both tyrannical and falsely known as democratic. Yarkpawollo was the first military officer who defected, took up arms, and terrorized the city of Monrovia, keeping the city at bay, locked down, school closures, etc. I was a kid in elementary school, and often, we were on lockdown until Yarkpawollo was killed, when according to the government, he was caught hiding in a palm tree with a loaded gun. He became a martyr.

Acknowledgments:

I am thankful to the editors of the following journals, magazines, and anthologies in which some of these poems or excerpts have previously appeared or are forthcoming:

The American Journal of Nursing (AJN); Harvard Review; Prairie Schooner; New Orleans Review; Newsday Magazine; Crab Orchard Review; Penn State Research Magazine; Transition Magazine: An International Review; Private: International Review of Photos and Texts; Sea Breeze Journal of Contemporary Liberian Writings; Common Wealth: Contemporary Poets on Pennsylvania; The Moon Day Reader; Encore Magazine; The Cortland Review; We Have Crossed Many Rivers: New Poetry from African, an Anthology; Asian Signature Series; Black Renaissance Noire; Connotation Press; Heart; Literary Orphans; The Enchanting Verses: Literary Review; RedLeaf Journal's African Diaspora Folio; The Literary Review; Journal of the African Literature Association (JALA); Prometeo Magazine; Chicken Bones: A Journal; Cutthroat, a Journal of the Arts; Truth to Power DoveTales: An International Journal of the Arts; The Missing Slate Magazine; Motherlines: Journal of the Motherhood Initiative for Research and Community Involvement; Grit and Grace: A Women Writing Anthology; The Tusculum Review.

I would like to thank the following people who have been of the greatest support to this project and to my work: Kwame Dawes, who gives himself so generously to Diaspora African writers like me, thanks to Michael Simms, who will never know how much he is appreciated, to Christine Stroud, and so many others out there for their continuous support, finally, to my four biological children, who put up with my using them as subject matter for poetry. What would I do without the tools we call children?

PATRICIA JABBEH WESLEY is the author of five collections of poetry, including *When the Wanderers Come Home, Where the Road Turns, The River Is Rising, Becoming Ebony,* and *Before the Palm Could Bloom: Poems of Africa.* Her work has appeared in numerous magazines, including *Harvard Review, Harvard Divinity Review, Transition Magazine, Prairie Schooner, Crab Orchard Review,* among others, and her work has been translated in Italian, Spanish, and Finnish. She teaches creative writing and African literature at Penn State Altoona.

New and Forthcoming Releases

Heartland Calamitous by Michael Credico

Voice Message by Katherine Barrett Swett
Winner of the 2019 Donald Justice Poetry Prize,
selected by Erica Dawson

The Gutter Spread Guide to Prayer by Eric Tran
Winner of the 2019 Rising Writer Prize,
selected by Stacey Waite

Praise Song for My Children: New and Selected Poems
by Patricia Jabbeh Wesley

under the aegis of a winged mind by makalani bandele
Winner of the 2019 Autumn House Poetry Prize,
selected by Cornelius Eady

Hallelujah Station by M. Randal O'Wain

Grimoire by Cherene Sherrard

Further News of Defeat: Stories by Michael X. Wang
Winner of the 2019 Autumn House Fiction Prize,
selected by Aimee Bender

Skull Cathedral: A Vestigial Anatomy by Melissa Wiley
Winner of the 2019 Autumn House Nonfiction Prize,
selected by Paul Lisicky

For our full catalog please visit: http://www.autumnhouse.org